wordless place

DEVOTIONAL POETRY

David Michael Lippman

Printed in the United States of America

Published by Soul-Care Press Inc.

Soul-Care Press Inc.
Santa Cruz, California
DavidMichaelLippman.com

Cover Design: Soul-Care.com
Cover Art: robpotter.media@gmail.com
Interior Art: J. Edward Designs
Original Package Design: Soul-Care Press Inc.

ISBN: 0998557724

First Edition

10 9 8 7 6 5 4 3 2 1

DEDICATION

Do you feel the world is broken? *(We do)*
Do you feel the shadows deepen? *(We do)*
But do you know that all the dark
won't stop the light from getting through? *(We do)*
Do you wish that you could see it all made new? *(We do)*

Is anyone worthy? Is anyone whole?
Is anyone able to break the seal and open the scroll?
The Lion of Judah who conquered the grave
He is David's root and the Lamb who died
To ransom the slave.

Is He worthy? Is He worthy?
Of all blessing and honor and glory
Is He worthy of this? He is.

- Andrew Peterson, *Is He Worthy?*

Songs, poems, even words themselves can touch us deep enough to draw out our truest longing, filling us with that joyful-ache for a world made right again—it is for this reason I write.

Two people have enflamed these longings most in me. Jesus, the one who made me, taught me, and while showing me, brought me to the Father on His shoulders.

And my wife, Keri, whose heart, soul, and hands have held mine as we pursue this beautiful journey with Him. I dedicate this book to you both.

Speak to Him thou for He hears, and Spirit
with Spirit can meet—

Closer is He than breathing, and nearer than
hands and feet.

> - Alfred Lord Tennyson,
> *The Higher Pantheism*

God keeps His holy mysteries
Just on the outside of man's dreams.

> - Elizabeth Barrett Browning,
> *Human Life's Mystery*

When that great Imagination which in the
beginning, for Its own delight and for the delight
of men…had invented and formed the whole
world of Nature, submitted to express Itself in
human speech, that speech should sometimes be
called poetry.

For poetry too is a little incarnation, giving body
to what had before been invisible and inaudible.

> -C. S. Lewis,
> *Reflections on the Psalms*

And now a very curious thing happened. None of the children knew who Aslan was any more than you do; but the moment Beaver had spoken these words everyone felt quite different.

Perhaps it has sometimes happened to you in a dream that someone says something which you don't understand but in the dream it feels as if it had some enormous meaning—either a terrifying one which turns the whole dream into a nightmare or else a lovely meaning too lovely to put into words, which makes the dream so beautiful that you remember it all your life and are always wishing you could get into the dream again.

It was like that now. At the name of Aslan each one of the children felt something jump in its inside.

C.S. Lewis,
The Lion, the Witch and the Wardrobe

CONTENTS

PREFACE

Poetry invites a connection and opens us to relationship. Somewhere inside the core of our being, our little artist operates the creative command center, pulling the levers, punching the switches, checking the data, and tugging our heartstrings. This poetic-heart delights in the authentic, bears our past experiences, yearns for truth, and pulses with future dreams. Though always present, the poetic-heart often articulates when everything else is silent and still.

Just as, by the shake of a hand, we can read and discern the impressions of another human being, so by the page, the ink, the rhythm and the rhyme, the author's poetic-heart encounters ours. The best poems whisper: "Come on in, friend, let us listen together."

The capacity for our poetic-heart to encounter another is integral to human flourishing. Without significant touch an infant will die; the aging soul never forgets this need. A million defenses, excuses, distractions, or hesitations might bar the way, but this inner mechanism toward relationship aches to create, to connect, to grow. But how?

Poetry can help express, even touch, some of those emotions, moments, and memories that overshadow our souls. Whether we're neglected, wounded, or just numb, spending time near the poetic-heart of another, like a fire, illumines the familiar face of our souls, nourishing that place of encounter, strengthening our personal, poetic-heart.

> You know everything I'm going to say before I start the first sentence. I look behind me and you're there, then up ahead and you're there, too—your reassuring presence, coming and going...
>
> Is there any place I can go to avoid your Spirit? You'd find me in a minute—you're already there waiting... "Oh, he even sees me in the dark! At night I'm immersed in the light!" It's a fact: darkness isn't dark to you; night and day, darkness and light, they're all the same to you.

Psalm 139. 4-7, 11-12

Moments spent in these encounters can run too deep for words, and, at times, may unearth the Author of life—the Creator *with* His created. When this relationship mingles with language, then prayer and poetry can unify into a single act of worship. As our attention turns to God's presence, our priorities shift, our perspective is shaped, our desires open, and our poetic-heart is made manifest. In literature this practice composes a somewhat neglected genre called *devotional poetry*. Poets like George Herbert, Gerard Manly Hopkins, Alfred Lord Tennyson, John Donne are lauded for craft though less recognized for their faith; while their works overflow with intimate expressions and profound experiences of living with the living God.

The Bible, too, is full of this sort of poetry. King David penned hundreds of poems in various seasons—each one a natural outflow of his relationship with God. The old testament prophets cried out in poetic-language, beautiful expressions of the human being worshipping its Creator. Jesus, the Son of God who we worship, memorized, discussed, and preached with Hebrew poetry. Because of Jesus, believers are called God's *poema*.[1] He animated kingdom realities with piercing spiritual metaphors. His Life brought new life, true life, to those ancient words.

Devotional poetry is an invitation for all of us to enter further into life *with* God. Getting honest. Getting vulnerable. Leaning in. Asking, in a moment of prayer, who is God to me right now? What is He doing in the midst of my heart? Dialoging those thoughts onto the surface, the skin, the lips. Letting the Word of God interact with our honesty.

So, let each of us return to our poetic-heart, our wordless place. It's not really about language at all, though language will assist us. It's a return to the heart of the passionate prophets, the Spirit of the song-writing king, the Object of the adoring priests, the questions of baffled Pharisees, the adoration of freshly pardoned prostitutes, and the open heart of the aching Author and prolific Perfecter of our faith. This is the place where authentic vulnerability nestles into ultimate Truth, an intimate connection of heaven and earth.

---

[1] Ephesians 2.10 – "For we are God's masterpiece." In Ancient Greek, masterpiece is *poiēma*, or poem, a created work from the Author of life.

Lucy buried her head in his mane to hide from his face.

But there must have been some magic in his mane. She could feel lion-strength going into her.

Quite suddenly she sat up.

"I'm sorry, Aslan," she said. "I'm ready now."

"Now you are a lioness," said Aslan. "And now all Narnia will be renewed."

- C.S. Lewis, *Prince Caspian*

COME

Prelude: The Quiet Man

Moraga Valley Presbyterian Church sits on a hill overlooking the valley and, as dusk sets in, fog creeps over the hills and blankets the homes. It was mid-season full-time ministry and the busy day just ended. Most of the staff already headed home. But I stayed a bit longer, sat on a table outside our youth offices and watched evening set in. Summer was fading fast and the cool breeze of autumn rustled through the leaves—a tangible sensation of changing seasons. A chill filled with longing for home, for returning, for rest.

As I watched the pace of nature, I sensed it was an invitation for me and for all who pay attention to their seasons to come and sit and slow and rest and be and become.

> And for all this, nature is never spent; there
> lives the dearest freshness deep down things;
>
> And though the last lights off the black West
> went oh, morning, at the brown brink
> eastward, springs—
>
> Because the Holy Ghost over the bent world
> broods with warm breast and with ah! bright
> wings.
>
> - Gerald Manly Hopkins, *God's Grandeur*

The Quiet Man

our summer settles
as the sun-rays paint the hills
from gold to a softer brown.

trees only half-lit,
flick the afternoon from their fingertips,
they primp and strip the bright day
for the night gown.

the matinee price is paid,
a grey blue sky reminds all who labor to cease;
and make whatever way one makes homeward.

twilight calls for silence,
tea or coffee with the inner man.
    what who said
    and why they said it
    become faded, and unimportant.
all is evening and all is bliss
when a single soul stops its march
    and waits on him,
    the quiet man, who meets with men,
    and makes them men.

Prelude: My Father's Clothes

Inside the entry of my parent's home, there once was a small closet full of old coats, jackets, and board games.

I clearly recall two items: my Dad's varsity jacket and his long trench coat from years working in Chicago. Neither item had been used since living in California. But something about them seemed timeless—a monument to years before me.

In the gospels, Jesus is baptized in the river Jordan, the heavens are rent open, and the Spirit descends on Him. The Father speaks these words:

> You are My beloved Son, in You I am well-pleased.
>
> -Luke 3.22

The Father makes this declaration of love and complete satisfaction in Jesus before He even did one recorded miracle. Only Jesus was perfectly fit to wear His Father's clothes, do His Father's work, fulfill His Father's goals. But even before Jesus fulfilled one public aspect of his ministry, God called Him "Beloved." That's just God's way. Usually we have it backwards.

My Father's Clothes

today i slipped on my father's coat,
a heavy weight with shoulders straight,
it hung down almost to my toes.

encloaked and wrapped, i wore his hat,
and sat and ate like him.
then i drank and thanked and sipped
and then i sipped again.

i waived a hand and wrote a check,
jotting down a scribbled note,
but all along it wasn't him
it was just my father's clothes.

so i tried to shout like him,
and then i called his friends,
at least with them i could act like him
but they know it's just pretend.

and i tasked to write like him
and sing like he would do,
yet i only wrote my name
and i only sang my tune.

so i tried to give like him,
i scraped and lost and bled,
i showed my love to others
but still they only said,

"that love, my boy, that looks like *you*,
and boy, we're sure to know,
'cause our suits 're worn in the same place,
we're only reaping what we've sown;

"sure, our lamplight's found an outlet
sure, it flutters in the wind,
but we're sure to keep it quiet 'n low,
so not to disturb the local residents.

"yes sir, the locals here, my son,
they're rough and rowdy crew,
careful not to get too close
or they'll have their way with you;

"betwixt the book and crooked path
there's a long and mountainous road,
but rare a man e're take that route
and ne're a bloke returneth home.

"we've a saying 'round these parts, my son,
that'll be a shield for your soul,
'don't dare ask the sordid questions
or you'll soil e'ry suit you own.'"

i hung my head and turned around,
i packed the clothes, finished the notes,
and gave my goals away.

only then as a naked boy
i heard my father return and say,

"oh, my son, where have you gone?
i've left behind my heavenly robe
to scour the towns, walk the mires,
and finally give the ghost;

"i've found my things scattered everywhere,
but where's the one that i love most?"

Prelude: Foolish

Israelite Wisdom Literature utilizes two major categories: the wise and the foolish. The wise understand that they're foolish in many things, and so seek wisdom. The foolish believe they are wise in many things, and thus reject wisdom.

Are we different? Look around. Before we even realize, foolish systems of thought and belief have been intricately imputed into our personal programming. This world was created to reveal God; every facet shaped to shine His face. But how often do we perceive Him as present, working, or good?

> A fool has said in his heart, "there is no God."
>
> - Psalm 14.1

Many times, our thoughts and actions can reveal a heart that says, "there is no God." How often do we live as if He's not actually around? "There is no God" is pasted and stapled on every realm of life. But there's another kind of fool:

> God chose what is foolish in the world to shame the wise.
>
> - 1 Corinthians 1.27

Foolish

a fool hath said in his heart "there is no God,"
and i have slept on winding trails
following a fool's words;

napping on rocks
hoping just one will be tough enough
to draw out a dream,

but heaven doesn't sleep in rocks
nor do winding trails unlock
the heart of God for us.

no, friend, "the fool hath said,"
and i swallowed whole his words
written in patterns
of streets and cars
of malls and shops
of books and songs
of candy and cough drops,

oh, that foolish word
spoken over me
wrapped within my infancy
when i was blind to influencing,
innocently incubating a foolish song
"neither right nor wrong;"
a fool's game played a fool's way,
a foolish dance on a foolish stage.

no, my God, i will no longer play,
enticing unbelief, toying
with half-veiled authenticity.

no, i am not a fool to You,
nor am i created to be,
but i am blood, i am body,
i am spirit and soul,
wounded and made whole;
fooled by the foolishness of fool-proof words,
a foolish face to fools
but no fool to the truth,
a fool full of the fullness of You;
and if i am foolish it's of benefit to You and you,

and if i seem foolish now
it's only a dream of heaven
breaking open in flesh unveiling,
bread broken, unleavened,
no, it doesn't bleed from rocks
nor lead through winding trails,
but as clouds rend, a voice once spoken
now opens over me, and i bend in praise
to the foolish One who says,

"this is My beloved son,
in whom I'm well pleased."

if i am a fool, Lord, then i am a fool for Thee.

The king's wrath terrifies like the roaring of a lion, but his favor is as [refreshing and nourishing as] dew on the grass.

- Proverbs 19.12 AMP

Prelude: Tired World

In an anxious society, exhaustion is all too familiar. It can be a battle just to slow down. And even when we do, we're confronted with layers of issues, regrets, disappointments and dreams that lie beneath the surface.

The whole of our existence, the land, the people, the nations, experience seasons of weariness. Some call it the daily grind. Others call it futility, meaninglessness, or an existential crisis. This poem enters into that desire to be restored, into the universal experience of weariness, and wonders: what does it look like to rest, recover, be still?

What would it look like for the world, inside and out, to slow down, take a deep breath, and begin to heal?

> For creation was subjected to futility, not willingly, but because of Him who subjected it,
>
> In hope that the creation itself will also be set free from its slavery to corruption into the freedom of the glory of the children of God.
>
> - Romans 8.20-21

Tired World

where does the earth sit when she feels tired?
is there an cosmic bench
on which she can breathe out
deep breaths from weariness?

where does earth rest
when trodden and worn down,
when the spinning arcing looping days
have worn long wrinkles
of brown and grey clouds
streaking north, south,
and every which way,
curves gnarled with age,
surface blemished,
atmosphere greyed?

when does the world ache her ache
and feel her weight?
can she give her wounds away
to the care of other worlds?
has saturn stretched its rings to her
or jupiter its moon
can mars cry red tears
or mercury sing a tune?
will the sun's rays warm her skin
when dawn breathes her early morn
(a reminder of that molten strength
boiling at the core)?

earth, your spinning face,
seems stern and wearing out

how and where and when and why
are questions full of doubt,

i wish to take your soiled form
and wash it white as snow,
yet there's only one place of endless rest—
maybe we both can go?

come play with me
among the rocks
among the scattered glass,
under you and under me
(looking for joyful-seriousness).

and like you do
(and you always do)
catch me in the in-between
i with you and you with me
in wordlessness and meaning;
a verity re-adjusting,
making men out of machinery,

turning head
tuning heart
shifting feet
'til pressure leaks out
as a steam engine wailing
and suddenly
like a runaway
we can breathe.

Prelude: The Discarded Garment

All humanity came from one simple breath of God. God breathed into dust and created Adam. Later, God would command Ezekiel to prophesy *breath* to the valley of dry bones, then His breath entered and brought life (Ezekiel 37.5). The Holy Spirit is often described as wind or breath, life-giving and sustaining. When *breath* comes, creation flourishes, when it leaves, creation disintegrates and dies.

> You take away their spirit, they expire and return to their dust. You send forth Your Spirit, they are created; and You renew the face of the ground.
>
> - Psalm 104.29-30

God isn't obligated to breathe on us. Nothing constrains Him to continue creating and sustaining us. His breath arises from His own perfect desire to love us. Despite all we've seen, still, He breathes.

> You laid earth's foundations a long time ago, and handcrafted the very heavens; You'll still be around when they're long gone, threadbare and discarded like an old suit of clothes. You'll throw them away like a worn-out coat, but year after year you're as good as new.
>
> - Psalm 102.23-28, *The Message*

The Discarded Garment

Father,
this life is
a garment
You are wearing
for a while, until
undressed and unfurled
You come naked upon this world.

all existence, a limp rag, spineless on the floor;
not even able to ask
for the life it's been given
not even able to breathe
without the body of God in it.

every threat is silent before this quiet tapestry,
wrinkled, worn and tossed
into an existential laundry;
for all things that were, are, and ever will be,
have been crumpled and washed
inside blood and timelessness—
the world, the mysteries,
every told and untold thing,
must be wrapped within Your presence
or truly cease to be.

(and my little sins
my quiet things
they are Yours
and You are breathing).

i will go 'til the hills hold no sound
and every mutter sends a ripple through,
trees and rocks and lakes bow down
to the verily unspoken rule;

all will mutter prayers like mine
that scatter through the grass
'til the winds run through 'ery blowing leaf
and brittle stalks lift up their heads.

Prelude: I am Just a Blade of Dry Grass

In our hallway hangs a brown frame containing a hand drawn picture of the small Rose of Sharon Prayer Chapel, where my wife, Keri, and I were engaged. Beneath the drawing is a handwritten poem—a memory from our years of dating.

We discovered this poem in a small coastal bookstore. While sipping mugs of tea, we explored the isles and stumbled on a small yellow book. Inside, we found words that spoke to what we had been through and where we were going.

It was a moment in time that beckoned a lifestyle:

> i am a little church (far from the frantic world
> with its rapture and anguish) at peace with
> nature
>
> —i do not worry if longer nights grow longest;
> i am not sorry when silence becomes singing
>
> winter by spring, i lift my diminutive spire to
> merciful Him Whose only now is forever:
> (welcoming humbly His light
> and proudly His darkness)

- e.e. cummings,
i am a little church(no great cathedral)

I am Just a Blade of Dry Grass

i am just a blade of dry grass
whispering through the wind,
i shutter and whisper, wait,
shutter 'n whisper again.

i am bending low listening
a blade, dry and parched
thin as a whisper i shutter 'n bend
with summer's windfilled art.

i am listening to my brothers
as they whisper low with me
bending now
listen to the ground,
to the song summerwind sings.

a song of summer
of sunlight aching
searching the earth
for surface to warm
something to touch
something, anyone, anything.

a blade of dry grass, dry as dry wind,
dry as dirt, dead as stone waiting, listening
bending on earth, bending for the something
the one thing that only absence makes known,

what is it the wind whispers to me?
what is it sunlight carries my way?

how they call in the whispers of my brothers.
how they call the earth from her slumber.

"the earth feels my ache," whispers the wind.
"the earth feels my scorch," whispers the sun.

and i am just a dry blade of grass
waiting for sundeath to come.

here i am, wind, heat, take me to what is next,
for i know nothing in this endless whisper,
this waiting, this wavedance of death.

but i will listen, i promise.
i do listen. i do.

i will believe, yes, i promise,
ah, summerwind, scorch me through.

i will wait. yes, i will.
here in this emptiness now,

'til the windwaves unravel
their forgotten promise.

'til summer unveils her valor.

Prelude: Bright Words

The Chronicles of Narnia. A Wrinkle in Time. The Velveteen Rabbit. Corduroy. The Giving Tree. Timeless books like these animate the beautiful exchange of relationship in the early years of innocence. Deep, significant connections occur in the precious childhood years. Yes, memories may fade, but something in our emotional DNA remains.

Maybe that's why God continually relates to us as children? Yes, we grow and mature into functioning adults but some part of us never grows up. Just as the Son of God never becomes the Father, neither do His offspring. There's a freedom in knowing that though we mature and grow, we never grow too old to be God's child.

> By the time you are Real, most of your hair has been loved off, and your eyes drop out and you get loose in the joints and very shabby.

> But these things don't matter at all, because once you are Real you can't be ugly, except to people who don't understand.

> *- The Velveteen Rabbit*

Bright Words

all men are like children,
aching for a playful spirit,
oh, we wait with a temper,
stomping and crying and asking,
and throwing our hearts against the wall;
'til bruising bones and broken skin,
reminds us of the readiness within,

as You lift felt tipped markers
of silver and gold; eternity and chaos
pressed against the flannel graph of our souls;
we attempt niceties, courtesy,
the kissing lips of a frenemy;

while Your fingers dabble in light
our shadow puppets bark and bite,
shouting voiceless cries to the nighttime;

oh, thrice You've illuminated and thrice we hide
in a game so forgotten that the slightest insight
could make our dreams alight
to fantasy once again.

and oh, that little child hiding within,
hiding there in the corner
who hears you writing
and runs, ever running, to find the Source;

between caves and stairways,
wardrobes and broken doors,
toward places only the heart's ever been before,

with a flick of the wrist,
the doorknob twists
and, oh my God,
too bright are the words,

as You step from the light
and in fatherly converse receive little me
into All-of-You,
and finally, we make-believe true.

Prelude: Love

The right kind of intimacy can bring deep freedom; a freedom to offer ourselves fully to another. But often our culture runs from any constraint upon free-will.

While working as a barista, one my fellow employees bragged about how many girls he was "with" while dating his current girlfriend. We began to discuss.

> "Stop? Why should I? I should be free to enjoy whomever, however."

> "But you lose something."

> "What?"

> "You lose the freedom to commit yourself fully to one person."

Love always carries a chain of commitment and consequences. God's love is always meant to bring us deeper into freedom.

> Now you are free from the power of sin and have become slaves of God…. All who are being led by the Spirit of God…are sons of God.

> - Romans 6.22; 8.14

Love

*Response to *A Homecoming* by Wendell Barry

all love is bondage.

chain links clanking, memories shaking their fist,
or the open palm receiving, lips pressed in a kiss,

love is lock and love is key;
one to give, one to receive.

aching souls long for chain linked love
to free us to be just and ever enough,
a glimmer together in the mirror of forever.

love is a long, slow unveiling;
for one a ship docked, for another a sailing.

have you found a heart you love without regret?
life without love is always meaningless;

love is a chain worn only around the neck.

oh, to be chained in love
is not loss to the longing soul.

love is a burden pure, clear, heavy as gold.

the only true pleasure
a fragmented world can offer.

love is a chain beyond the coffin;
pleasure or poison, but never an option.

so won't you sit and sip with me,
as love's heavy chains enjoin everything?

won't you drink to the dregs the heaviest weight,
glory and light-filled, heavy, intoxicating,
with you and me, and all humanity,
draped together, in love, enchained forever;

as the promise to stay
slays the freedom to leave
with a sword of gold
and the jewels of peace,

ships n' sails full and flying,
coffins open, dead undying,
the chest is open,
no need for they key,

love will ever always be
a bondage of becoming.

i do not think i've found
this place that you have gone
i've climbed over the mountains
i've searched over the dawn
i've traced my steps to hell
i've wandered o'er seas
yet, o Jesus, where you wander
still seems dark to me.

i've clamored over bookends
i've scaled education
i've lost a lot of friends
i've met with every nation
and still i'm looking for
this place of quiet rest,
Jesus, won't you come
and show me where it is?

Prelude: **I Took My Sandals Off**

I took the first steps into my room during a silent retreat in Big Sur, CA. It'd been awhile since I'd gone away just to be with Jesus. I needed it.

The room was simple, and the view was gorgeous. A sliding glass door opened to a private view of the Pacific Ocean. Wow, marvelous. My spirit began to breathe. My shoulders relaxed. I slipped my sandals off and put my things on the floor.

I leaned on the wall and opened my hands.

To let go of the day-to-day.

To begin to let my soul out of its cage.

Even as I write this I can remember. And it stills my soul. The smell of the sea. The warm air. The sunlight on oak trees.

I was drawn into rest. The expanse of the ocean became a canvas for God's handiwork. My room became holy ground. Sacred space for me and Jesus to meet.

These lyrics leapt out of my pen and into my journal, moments of quiet captured forever.

I Took My Sandals Off

i took my sandals off and i touched the walls
thanking You for Your presence
and asking Your protection,
loving affection, and timeless resurrection;

as the sea side became a more brilliant hue
than the bluest blue i was ever used to,
i wanted to gather it into my arms
by the loadfull
and hold it 'til
sunlight carried
the molecules
and me back
back back
to its home
among the white of white clouds

where i would wander with water
through that windy way
that makes all men brave,
washed, clean, and save face,

but no, no, not yet, it's always as though,
through the narrows, through the gate,
the thirsty must go;

and bend and follow light's open eye,
not blinking, but keeping, wading, unhiding
'til those with souls only fully alive
can bound into the river full and wide,

and ride the Ghost giving, giving, and given,
into the estuary winding, flooding the canyon,
'til every crevice and crack, cave and question,
dirt and doubt is drenched 'n sopping
with the fragrance of heaven.

Look at him, crouched like a lion, king of beasts; who dares mess with him?

The scepter shall not leave Judah; he'll keep a firm grip on the command staff…

He will wash his shirt in wine and his cloak in the blood of grapes, his eyes will be darker than wine, his teeth whiter than milk.

- Genesis 49.8-12, *MSG*

Prelude: **Sympathy**

We all encounter pain and struggle. We all face temptation and fear. Is God at work in these? And how? And why do those seem hardest to speak with Him about?

> For we do not have a high priest who cannot sympathize with our weaknesses, but One who has been tempted in all things as we are, yet without sin.
>
> > - Hebrews 4.15

Empathy is a popular word in our culture while sympathy is forgotten inside the thin walls of Hallmark. But the word *sumpathēsai* used in Hebrews 4.15 means to have fellow-feeling with.[2] It's root is *sumpathés*, which means *suffering with* another. It's the action of Jesus in the present Spirit of God, the Spirit groans within us because He is intimately acquainted with *all* of our ways (Rm 8.26; Ps 139.3)

The Message Bible writes it this way:

> We don't have a priest who is out of touch with our reality. He's been through weakness and testing, experienced it all—all but the sin. So let's walk right up to him and get what he is so ready to give.

---

[2] http://biblehub.com/lexicon/hebrews/4-15.htm

Sympathy

only You can sympathize truly,
knowing all of me,
the temptation to look at myself
and hold my empty cup against Your wealth,

yes, only You can sympathize truly
for You wore flesh fully,
in perfect unity with the Spirit of life
trapped inside Your chest,
You unleashed overflowing love
into me, spilling Your breath;

for only You can sympathize truly
You know dually, both infinite and me,
both divine and fleshy,
taking form of God
and folding, stuffing, boxing tight into skin,
wearing my limbs, feeling my weakness
knowing my temptations,
holding my broken relations;

when i was cold as coal,
what fire You held;
as the world tore Your flesh
unleashing God's fire through God-forsaken,
so willingly, my sin intaken,
checked the box: now legal in heaven,
no, no, i'm not misktaken on this,
somehow, some way, i have *Your* righteousness?

held between Your wings now,
in a beloved-strong tied,
with ropes of God three chorded,
wrath unraveled; and out your wounded side
spill lovingkindness and sorrow ever for me?
yes, forever sown into Your life, the King.

one look upon my pain?
You burst with compassion
with nothing to gain, eyes past my reluctance
of a shared resurrection; my flesh in Your cross,
my gain, Your loss; never losing perspective,
Your will, my thoughts; transformed, directed.

and i whisper this now
but someday You'll shout it
to the nations, to the world,
to all who love it or doubt it;
and those secrets, yes, even my littlest shames
unshaken, stilled, calmed, claimed,
in the ever-present love, the infinite by and by,
of your unashamed, unblinking,
ever-sparkling eye.

"if" and "when" are unremembered questions
as Your divine hand keeps pouring and pouring
resurrection upon resurrection upon resurrection
inside the same me inside the same You;
every-always You'll show me
how i ever-always knew; i knew, i knew, i *knew*
i knew You all along; You who always,
how You will always, always prove,
Jesus, You alone, sympathize me true.

a good book with holes is no good book.

*a well-meaning phrase riddled with knives
is not safe.*

*a poem hammered flat with a gavel
holds no room for you or me.*

*an eardrum hard as clay
makes no noise and no home for guests.*

a fire can purify or destroy.

fight fire with fire, i say.

a good book with holes is no good book.

Prelude: Fridge Poem II

On a road trip across country with my future wife, I happened upon a refrigerator with a cluster of word magnets. Perfect introvert moment.

My first poem was lost, but *Fridge Poem II* was better anyway. These words still come back to me from time to time. A surprising moment of invitation amidst busyness and adventure.

How often since then I've looked past these sorts of moments?

Still God provides continual invitations. Inviting us to experience heaven, to be touched by glory, to walk into His presence in a quiet moment of unveiling.

> Earth's crammed with heaven
> And every common bush afire with God
> But only he who sees, takes off his shoes,
> The rest sit round it and pick blackberries,
> And daub their natural faces unaware.
>
> - Elizabeth Barret Browning

Fridge Poem II

heaven
must be
some clothes
you can feel—
like somewhere
nearby
you wouldn't look.
oh make
heaven
where you put
your heart
only
looking
there from
the night.
can you get
at me,
your love,
to know me,
that place
i have been?
"smile stunning
little one
it is
Mine
look in."

It would seem that Our Lord finds our desires not too strong, but too weak.

We are half-hearted creatures, fooling about with drink and sex and ambition when infinite joy is offered us, like an ignorant child who wants to go on making mud pies in a slum because he cannot imagine what is meant by the offer of a holiday at the sea.

We are far too easily pleased.

- C.S. Lewis, *The Weight of Glory*

Prelude: Threaded In

The human eye naturally draws lines from point to point. From constellations, to art, to mathematics, our brain is created to follow dots, angles, curves, and form perspectives that create reality.

This is true also of our souls. We are attached creatures. We attach to our caretakers. We attach to dreams and hopes. We attach to societal movements, institutions, and culture. We attach to our belief systems, religions, and practices. Even our souls are eclipsed by grander attachments: world history, common sense, meaning, morality and its consequences. How we connect to these ultimate "dots" creates our reality and the story of our soul. These connections can give us a glimpse of wisdom, a taste of reality. Jesus said,

> You shall know the truth, and the truth shall make you free.

The Greek word for truth here isn't *logos*, which was commonly used, but *aletheia*—which means *reality*.[3] *Aletheia* was synonymous for the opposite of illusion. Glimpse of reality, true reality, and reality will set you free.

---

[3]https://www.blueletterbible.org/lang/lexicon/lexicon.cfm?t=kjv&strongs=g225

Threaded In

have you ever seen
how the world is tied
to you and me with strings
spun of memory, anger,
hopes and dreams, themes upon themes,
vibrating together like violin strings,
a constant melody,
humming beauty and dissonance
according to the variance
of everyday orchestry?

are we pushed or pulled or dragged along?
or strung n' left limp as puppets forgotten?

and i can barely glimpse the string's end
does it reach beyond the years?
and i can scarcely hope its finding
though i shed its tears,
and beyond, it's my reminding,
can i never know it here?
yet i'm wondering
and i'm finding

if it's You that threads me in.

softened air
once warmed by light
is delight
to a stubborn soul
waiting whole winters
alone inside,

yes, even those who hibernate
eventually come awake.

Prelude: Seed & Spire

Seeds seem insignificant. But once planted, they begin to open in the dark, nourished by water and nutrients human eyes rarely glimpse.

> For you have been born again not of seed which is perishable but imperishable, that is, through the living and enduring word of God.
>
> - 1 Peter 1.23

We already know how seeds on earth function. But what about seeds from heaven? Is a seed given from God is full of divine DNA (2 Peter 1.4)?

God's seed implanted grows in the darkness of our souls, the deepest places. As it germinates, its roots reach into the unseen nutrients of His presence. Without roots we won't survive. And God's seed is stranger still. Its shoots confront, engage, ache-further, and love-in the hardest of soils. Its bloom doesn't remain static but becomes a beautiful sign of the awakened soul, the heart alive, the self-aware.

> The seed is in the ground
> Now may we rest in hope
> As darkness does its work.
>
> - Wendell Berry

Seed & Spire

implanted word,
faith seed from where
the encasing of the world is torn away,
an unraveled shell shed for nutrients,
as stagnancy gives way softening.

tendrils reach higher and higher
spires press through mire,
stabbing night, poking holes
into a black veil ceiling,
darkness revealing, earth warming.

i reach, reach, reach, o why,
why, why must Your clues
be so hard to find
for so many?
and me.

i am breaking the edge
birthed through earth,
kneading the surface,
i breathe and ache and bend
and bloom in the bleary daybright.

i yawn forgetting the night
that nourished me down below
and still drinking deep, my life to keep
in that river's hidden flow;
waking, i rise, unto faces like mine
flowered and flourished in the great sunlight.

Batter my heart, three person'd God; for,
you as yet but knock, breathe, shine,
and seek to mend;
That I may rise, and stand,
o'erthrow me, and bend Your force,
to break, blow, burn and make me new.

- John Donne, *Holy Sonnet XIV*

my stream is a prayer
water flows from who knows where
water goes where it goes
my stream is a prayer only you know

my stream is a prayer with words unknown
water babbles like a baby
waters skips and flows
my stream is a prayer of joyful sorrow

my stream is a prayer of unending reflection
water sings of secret ways
water knows unending days
my stream is a path through the quiet place

my stream is a lilting love of one
water flows without any resistance
water bubbles and dances in its rhythm
my stream is a private depth of communion

my stream is a prayer of unending days
water flows unstoppable unforced unclaimed
water sings with or without an ear
my stream is a prayer
and you are drawing near.

KNOW

Prelude: Steadfast. Immovable

I penned this series of eleven meditations in 2010 during transition from full-time work into marriage. These were written all throughout California—whether in Tahoe cabins or suburban homes, I began to discover God's presence in the everyday uncertainties.

I hoped to experience God shepherding my heart as I left one role and location and move into a deeper one. First Corinthians 15.58 commands us to,

> Be steadfast, immovable, always abounding in the work of the Lord, knowing that your toil is not in vain.

How can we be steadfast, immovable? As I pondered Jesus, His love, His power, His life, it began to strengthen my resolve. This transition was one of the hardest and best in my life. These poems are a glimpse of how constant and strong He is, even when we can't see what lies ahead.

> Jesus Christ is the same yesterday, today and forever.
>
> - Hebrews 13.8

I. Christ Steadfast. Immovable.

Christ steadfast. immovable.
grace standing beside you, alive.
an eternity of confidence,
our obedience
through his death, our life—
a world maker,
and he's on our side!
we are bound to him,
by irremovable love
       perfect desire,
       sure wisdom,
       calm power,
you may have thought
you lay down with a lamb,
yet you awaken
with your hand in his mane
and lion breath on your face.

II. Christ Steadfast. Immovable.

Christ steadfast. immovable.
holding every heartbeat
and the length of every soul.

love sounds his call (in silence),
it echoes past the mind
between ribs and organs,
it presses an eternal weight
upon the chest-depth
unknown in every man;

yes, stars shine
the ocean crashes
a baby cries
and Christ—he dances!

what a clap, a romp,
an endless celebration
for the rock is seated
and his throne is creation.

III. Christ Steadfast. Immovable.

Christ steadfast. immovable.
a thousand fingers point to you,
attentively reflecting
your attention and your truth;
an outpouring of love, adoration,
a love-song through and through;
a new love-song for every generation,
hummed from a never-ending tune.

interceding, proclaiming,
you're overcoming our fears;
you've enlaced our Father's hand
with ours, our stories, our years;
you share your desire,
motives pure, light entwined,
you speak of the future,
with a gleam in your eye.
sing, dangerous one,
sing, for death and life again,
speak the freedom in spirit and truth
that you spoke flesh-wrapped in
the life-breath, the fragrance,
the sign that all men might live,
the odor of our tears,
the guarantee of the fullness;
our forever-shared inheritance.

oh, dearest, Jesus, thank you,
despite the graces we forget,
here's to the hope of the future
you're making for us yet.

determination makes a man
in this world of mechanism,
so what things can't i avoid
by internal segregation?
bittered shards of broken stone stand
stacked as my testimony;
built by our modern matrimony
of achievement and safety—

these messy hands have lost all touch
inanimately stacking and stacking
while life is growing all around us.

IV. Christ Steadfast. Immovable.

Christ steadfast. immovable.
unending glorious weight;
inked blood upon our heart
he wrote secrets in our cage;

our essence more him than us,
our fears, more his than ours,
our hope, life alone in him,
our passions inside his heart;
his robe, our only covering,
his smile, our daily bread,
the weight within us lifted;
he's first of the living dead.

the fire within us burns
from the twinkle in his eye—
it melts our souls,
and we shiver
inside rivers of delight,
we splash in joy,
we swim in grace,
oh, we drink deep his love,
we breath in hope
it sings like life,
that final, long satisfaction,

we play in peace and sell our things
only to buy the only bread
that ever tasted like broken life
and split the heart of heaven.

V. Christ Steadfast. Immovable.

Christ steadfast. immovable.
overcoming love that overcame.
the conqueror, the victor, still stands
close to the peasant, touching the slave;
shutting perdition, deception
and death in his grave.

now the addict renews
into a sweeter addiction,
a beloved devotion
to the floodlight of heaven.
oh, we've written it now,
yet it's outside our skin
and somehow still
written somewhere within;

oh, secret men ache for,
deity touching men still,
from the heights of heaven
to the dry rot of hell,
from the ache of the homeless
to the wanderer on the sea,
to the endless hesitation
in the ocean of the deceived,

how can you, Jesus, not be working,
for isn't somewhere deep within
sounding still that word you spoke
when beginning began to begin?

VI. Christ Steadfast. Immovable.

Christ steadfast. immovable.
invisible joy piercing hearts;
heart-pierced with songs of innocence
rekindled, united, set apart.

yes, serendipity, she's nice;
and providence, he's okay;
fate is a man of action;
and with luck, it's anyone's game;
but honestly, i'd rather wait
trapped in Your endless love,
wrapped in a God-sized satisfaction,
surrounded, known, touched.
can't i just sing with you
while you sing over me?
can't i just dream
a dream you made for me?
can't i just pause
and talk with you awhile?
can't i just be quiet
inside your quiet smile?
may i dance and twirl,
with the moments and the worlds?
may i stop and sing
of the story that you're writing?
may i meet you there
in the beauty and despair,
and stay with you my alien maker,
my humbled, foreign ambassador,
my playful, light-filled forgiver,
my eternal, inseparable redeemer?

i don't want to be in hiding anymore
my lord, my lord
i don't want to be in hiding anymore
and i'm tired of making
all my excuses
try to stand,

ignore my ignorance, Jesus
and repeat in me the work
done through you
my innocence is through
my fire's out, my life is blind,
my way is wayward
without you.

i don't want to be in hiding anymore,
i will stop the lies;
i give you my rebel heart
and wait here in the light.

VII. Christ Steadfast. Immovable.

Christ steadfast. immovable.
sun of righteousness risen high like noon
so apart yet so a part of everything we do.

i do not eat but what you give,
i do not breath but that you live,
i do not live but that you rise,
i do not rise but that you abide
                              with me.

come to Christ my soul. come once again.

my skin-weaver,
a heart-beater,
a world once shared,
now breathing your air,
we claim you now,
to find and be found out.

heart-light in men,
come near us again,
make haste, that we
may drink ever deep
your sweetlight;
for i close my eyes
and fear once again,
only you make everything alright,
my friend.

VIII. Christ Steadfast. Immovable.

Christ steadfast. immovable.
a much deeper devotion, oh God
in you, the word within,
just one prayer
and the silence rumbles
with your wonderful will;
and i am among those stretched
lost and looped,
captured and indwelt by you!
oh come on, God,
all that you are is in me?
did you make me big enough
to hold all eternity?
this is a mad man's lyric
an anxious oxymoron
yet so met and sense-filled
with the resonance of this otherworld.
i find joy beneath you
love in your vast humility
so a-part
it's a part of all of me,
so beyond
that it explodes in erratic colors
unsearchable joys
unknowable tastes
undeniable graces
that make up to-day,
you are so satisfied with all your ways
in me: your fumbling, God-filled, idiot.

IX. Christ Steadfast. Immovable.

Christ steadfast. immovable.
i come in on Your shoulders,
i eat light,
i resound with peace,
i ask, and it is given,
i sing with you, i sing.

our fellowship on your initiation:
my soul weeps and laughs,
our fragrance in the courts,
dressed in elegance, we dance,
among the pillars, upon the throne,
and i sit up in your lap, and oh so fast
we ride to a sleepless land,
in your garments
i am wrapped,
i breathe in and relax
forever love is given;
your heartbeat is my heaven.

"how precious you are to me."
my heart beats back to yours

"how very precious, my son,"
and i hear that we are one.

when you are God, then what am i?
oh, so glad to be nothing
but caught up in your light.

X. Christ Steadfast. Immovable.

Christ steadfast. immovable.
i swear i'm addicted to your perfection
i can be completely human
my full-mess,
my whole-imperfection;
because you're heaven's joy
unshakable light,
a powerful vibrato shaking the night
is your necessary immanence with me
mind shattering moments draped
in silence so loud it presses
through every thought, emotion,
fear or hope to constant eternity,
your spirit in mine
through mine, over me,
your terrifying presence
never ever to harm me
can i take it? no, no.
it's my joy to die
my hope accomplished inside
through your perfect satisfaction
your own tri-union,
i am finally made light,
an undone confession,
an open adoration
oh, my Jesus, Jesus,
how i love Thee
how i've proved you o're and o're
Jesus, Jesus precious Jesus,
oh for grace to know you more.

XI. Christ Steadfast. Immovable.

adore. the foundation that molds all life

adore. the revealing light, which even
darkness cannot hide

adore. the unspeakable weight and
heaviness, a love that lasts forever

adore. the person that embraces every
spirit of man and woman

adore. the devotion and endurance of this
love

adore. the wisdom by which he dresses
and undresses all

adore. the way in which he does all things

adore. the unity of these in Jesus Christ
steadfast. immoving.

I wept and wept and wept that no one was found able to open the scroll, able to read it.

One of the Elders said, "Don't weep. Look—the Lion from Tribe Judah, the Root of David's Tree, has conquered.

He can open the scroll, can rip through the seven seals."

- Revelation 5.4-5, *MSG*

Prelude: From the Beginning

Rose of Sharon Prayer Chapel at Biola University sits between a three-story library and a busy street. Thousands of students pass by its unassuming bricks and lackluster steeple on a daily basis—its doors always stay open, twenty-four-seven.

Built in 1966, the chapel remains the oldest chapel on campus. No events are ever held here—it is a quiet place specifically set apart for prayer.

As a student, this quiet sanctuary became solace amid the busy dorms and high academics of college. In class, my mind bubbled over with wonderful thoughts of God, but Rose of Sharon was where I learned to love Him.

It is in these places of encounter that God opens our minds and looks in. Suddenly, we glimpse a revelation of His eyes, His thoughts, His love. He still speaks today.

> In these last days has spoken to us in His Son, whom He appointed heir of all things, through whom also He made the world. And He is the radiance of His glory and the exact representation of His nature, and upholds all things by the word of His power.
>
> - Hebrews 1.2-3

From the Beginning

when i consider who You are within little me
and how full You are containing little me,
i must bow to the heir of all things
to the Maker to Whom i am returning.

now You, the Final Word
speaking now through vocal cords,
saying things like "count the cost;
is it worth it to gain the world
and watch your soul be lost?
store up treasure where moth and rust
will not destroy
no, no thief or devil can steal
heavenly joy.

now i hear, "even the spheres,
spinning like records round a star,
their time, place, near and far
is according to Me.
for should I choose,
I could wear them like jewelry,
dangle jupiter, mars, neptune on a string,
letting their vibrating beauty extol Me
(as it should be);
I chose rather to give them names,
treat them like sheep whom
I lead in and out again.

can you number them?
can you tell if one is missing?

I shepherd them to quiet streams, yes,
even little infinite things like these.

"could it be,
that you would think to comprehend Me?"
as my ears ring with prophesy,
"don't you see?
this was My genius: I founded *you*.
(not the other way 'round)
with bleeding hands,
bruised chin,
unbroken bones,
crying breath,
I found you out—
and you thought I was hidden?

I came to you,
from unimaginable heights
to incomprehensible depths,
I shrank,
becoming little
without becoming less.
do you not see this was easy for Me?
it's My world; I'll do as I please.
I am the fashioner,
a world-maker,
I breathe divine glory;
a word from My lips and I rewrite your story,
things begin or cease,
the incomprehensible written into
comprehending,

(and you thought *you* found Me?)
even when I carried the cross—
I still carried the worlds in my pocket.

still my spirit stirs, "was it a rouse
that no one came to my rescue?
that by My command
thousands of jealous angels
didn't come in and tear this world to shreds?
(and did you think this allowed
 a sort of indifference to sin
that you could come
and 'ask *Me* in?')

"oh, child, I came unbidden,
unwanted, like a lamb led to slaughter
by a love-drunk father, a shepherd to His alter,
just one match—a spark—now I burn forever,
all authority, all power, all glory, all together
with your hand in mine, we'll rewrite time,
unravel terrors of night, and dream
a dream of a dream once forgotten
once remembered, once reborn, twice forgiven
thrice beloved, thrice entwined, thrice enthralled,
thrice made Mine,
thrice and once just a way between
the great hallway of love to the throne of King"

thrice He smiles, yes, my ears still ring;
"don't think for a moment, child, you found Me:
this was all My idea from the beginning."

Prelude: Glory

Jacob slept on the dirt. His head rested upon a rock.

A runaway. His brother's heart broken. His mother's words lingering in his ears. His father's blessing upon him. Regret curdling in his stomach.

Was this the life he'd chosen? Was this his so-called blessing?

Sometimes God's path leads us down unfamiliar and uncomfortable trails, it can even seem like He's absent. David, after being anointed as king, spent 14 years running for his life, sleeping in caves. Joseph too had prophetic dreams of political leadership, instead he became a slave and a prisoner. God has cloaked his glory on earth in a veil of everyday. But Jacob's story didn't end there, neither did Joseph's, nor David's, nor yours.

> Then Jacob awoke from his sleep and said, "Surely the Lord is in this place, and I did not know it."
>
> He was afraid and said, "How awesome is this place! This is none other than the house of God, and this is the gate of heaven."
>
> - Genesis 28.6-7

I. Glory

Jesus, you are searching and you are finding
all the secrets that open us
open heaven.
let angelic presences
worship around us,
let glory weigh in on our shoulders,
let coats of glory replace the weight of weary
over and over and over; for
to be yoked to you
no longer means
to join in a crucifixion
but joining in your everlasting body
that wears my scars eternally.

i watch as
bright eyes
shine in darkness
radiating 'til all the fullness of deity
is manifest on earthly soil.

we cannot extract divinity from dirt;
fingerprints still pulse beneath the earth.

is it any surprise then
that the hearts of men
make chaos out of glory?
we seem to make our way in a world of dark
not knowing our inner story;
bonded to a voice half-recognized
as fate and futility
meaningless toil and destiny.

as rivers of blood flow over our feet
washing clean what we could never clean
and unleashing love in unbeckoned generosity,

ever longing for light
to turn the phrase long forgot,
longing to be healed,
longing to be clean,
longing to be forgiven,
for living in a bleak world.

glory isn't glorious for me
until it's unfurled.

glory urges us all to be revealed.

II. Glory

in fluttering wings
heaven breathes on me softly
and i do whisper back
though i don't know
the words

fog punches holes
through twilight's gaze
singing over me quietly, heaven
comes like a cloud-fire
letting in and out the light
through me

bitter wind pulls
hair back on my skin
shivers of my own voice cast
shadows over starlight holes
and i am pulling myself down
through this

enveloped in nighttime
well, the heavens shine inside
and sink in wondering eyes—
no face is given heaven
please see me through this.

III. Glory

i take comfort in the fact
that heaven's eyes are open wide
breathlessly backward
seeking all of the earth
and i can't help but wonder
where am i in heaven's gaze?
when angels peek in, what secret lives
do the angels hold steady, anxious,
o'er the children of men?

i am not who you say i am.
i do not even let that voice
speak to me anymore.
nor am i who i say i am,
nor angels, nor demons,
nor things present, nor things to come
no, i am a homebody now,
wrapped in linens bled white,
wrapped in veils torn in two,
yes, i agree with the only voice i hear anymore
yes, my friend, my father, yes
heaven is open.

One vital quality which [the great saints] had in common was *spiritual receptivity*. Something in them was open to heaven, something which urged them Godward…

They had a spiritual awareness and they went on to cultivate it until it became the biggest thing in their lives.

They differed from the average person in that when they felt the inward longing they *did something about it.*

They acquired the lifelong habit of spiritual response.

- A.W. Tozer, *The Pursuit of God*

Prelude: **Did He Know?**

Every summer I worked on staff at Redwood
Camp, the director started our staff training with
washing each other's feet. And camp-feet are rarely
clean.

Someone would play guitar. Two by two we'd
approach the wash basin and clean the grime off
each other with water and a towel. Gorgeous
Redwood trees towered above. Streams trickled
by. Soon flocks of campers would arrive. There
would be significant relationships, comradery,
connection.

Years later, I proposed to one of those counselors,
and we washed each other's feet. Months later we
were wed. At our ceremony, she washed my feet
and I washed hers. Through ups and downs, highs
and lows, trials and joys, sometimes still, we will
slow down, just to remember and wash each
other's feet once again.

> [Jesus] rose from supper. He laid aside his outer
> garments, and taking a towel, tied it around his
> waist. Then he poured water into a basin and
> began to wash the disciples' feet and to wipe
> them with the towel that was wrapped around
> him.

> - John 13.2-5

Did He Know?

what did Jesus know when he stripped his clothes
and girded in a towel
smirked with a servant's smile?

what did he know
as water trickled through his fingers
smeared with grime and sweat?
did he watch the darkened liquid
race over his hands
and burrow in the cracks
of calices worn from years
of labor in his father's shop?

did he hesitate
when fragrances of earthworn feet
trailed past his bearded face
and drown in his nostrils?

did his heart race as layers of dirt
and filth, built for days and days
soaked, cracked, and simply wiped away?
is that how he could smile
at the pebble-of-the-church's bipolar requests
commanding with a question,
pressing against this potent action?

and did his heart race when he kneeled low
before the face of one now given wholly
over in his mind to the devil in disguise?

did Jesus quibble?
did he pause and wring the cloth,
letting each brown drop plink-plink-plank
into the bowl, counting the cost,
waiting and washing, washing and waiting,
for a murmur, a whimper,
just a whisper from his poisoned brother?

did each liquid ripple remind him
of the cup of thick black wine
fragrant, rotten, sopping
with the filth of all mankind?
did he realize, even now,
what horror it would be
to lift and sip and down the whole thing
spirit, soul, body,
til it wrenched
inside, seared like fire through his veins;

taking him down, down, down,
yes, down to the lowest place;
beyond even the bearded faces
of nominal tradesmen;
beyond wealth stolen by the dirty and desperate;
beyond tombs washed in white;
and tears bleeding from the corners
of the whore's swollen eyes;
beyond space, beyond time,
beyond broken ladders in the race toward heaven,
beyond the bent bondage of kings like herod,
as pharaohs upon pharaohs upon pharaohs
who no matter how long you'd plague 'em
sayin' 'let my people go'

there'd never be a curse fierce enough
to break the heart of unfeeling,
unloving, unopened?

and oh, did Jesus recall that desert moment
just before hunger struck him
when man's inhumanity to man
leaned thrice on his shoulder
and whispered the one word
by which he might escape this putrid fate
of sipping deathwater?
if only, if only, if only he'd taken that offering
a mere three years ago—

one knee, that's all it would've taken, just one,
maybe not even a knee
just a nod, a gulp,
a slouch of his shoulders,
maybe after being deprived
of touch, of food, of help,
that very hour
with barely a word
he could've breathed away
this fragrant fate wafting in his face?

it could've been so easy, so fast,
the most efficient way to get the kingdom going,
get those keys and get the world growing again,
while ever-knowing the fate of man
would lay fettered to the wrists of no human.

no, no, what he knew then he knew now,
he knew it three years deeper and so familiar
with man's inhumanity, and who it was that tore
the soul so pure, entangling it with insanity,
in handcuffs of silver and gold,
promises unmade, cajoled,
the light of the godhead
darkened just enough
to curse the world he created
for a serpent and a son
for a battle lost to become a battle one
with deathwater dripping,
aromas of sweat and feces and failure
rising from dirt, breath still trapped inside earth.

and i wonder now,
if he swallowed hard and opened his ear
to hear that Voice in the garden
who drawing near
with a cup darker even than blood
personally denied the request
of the only Son of God,
sending angels instead to strengthen
the body and the soul
for when flesh is weak the spirit is full
of potential aching, shaking like the ripples
forming in water
dripping down his wrists
and splashing on the floor
of an ordinary room
in this late hour,

where the scents of lamb and bitter herbs
wafted over befuddled men's beards
as they watched him undress
his cloak and sash
and in nakedness
wrap himself with the garments
of an ordinary servant
and smirk at the guests of his private banquet,
and the billions of faces those twelve represented;
was it anything to him to bow before the chosen,
and ache with the broken,
and wash the dirt once stolen
from the feet of adam,
lifted by his hand and touched, and held,
and known in this moment.

did Jesus cower, cajole, gripe or complain?
did he grimace, or sneer, or huff, or gag?
did he pause to consider
or did he already know,
what the blood and that body
could become when dipped low
in the blackest wrath
from his friends' skin and soul
speaking a lesson still being glimpsed
and given over
and over and over
and over and over again?

"you do not realize now," he said,
"but you shall understand," and he bent,
and he bared, and he washed, and endured
with full obedience, knowing the smell, the faces,

the pigment of those whom God embraced
and gave to him.

he stepped into something
we're only beginning to glimpse;
those who felt the touch of his hand,
the sound of his voice,
and watched him bow low,
spoke of this moment
only in whispers (and shouts)—
for now, you and i can only wonder with them,
our dear Jesus, what did You know?

i am never far
from my broken heart
tethered together
in mary's arms

Prelude: Barricade

In the middle of suburbia there's a dry reservoir with a useless dam. For months, I would jog by this empty barrier and began to wonder, what was this wasteland like when it was filled? It's not often you can stand at the base of a dam without the imminent threat of being crushed. My imagination burst with a vision of the barricade breaking and a deluge rushing over suburbia.

Luckily for them, that well was dry. But in our spiritual lives sometimes we have to let things open-up, let the river flow out. Our practices, our liturgies, our cultural influences, our society pressures, and our high achievements can protect us from the abundant life and relationship God has placed inside us. Our souls become small eddies rather than estuaries.

We live with longings too deep for words. We can spend our lives avoiding situations where we could naturally open up. In some cases, this is a self-protective gift from God. But someday soon our souls will need to unload. The prayer closet. The confessional. The alter. The coffee shop. The journal. It doesn't matter. Just remember: let your soul out with God and with others. Otherwise we'll remain stagnant as a dry reservoir in suburbia.

Barricade

but when the whole sea flowed down
breaking the barricade and flooding in
wave upon wave upon wave upon wave
as trees bent, walls break,
the land shook and the air split
making way making way for the infinite depths—

sounds of clapping and stomping, cracking, snapping,
many voices shouting together—oh, oh the agony of forever;

cries of children clutching mother's promises
long life, big dreams,
n' who-knows-what-you'll-make-of-things,
until all is swept deep underneath
thrashing for air, breaking surface into screaming,
thrust beneath with a gulp—no longer breathing;
stretching lungs as burning coals, bulging eyes,
grasping life, "oh, Jesus Christ!"
our fight to survive disintegrates, divides,
drowns and dies, letting love break into the lies
                              we've been living in—

it's like waking up underwater,
in an undersea war,
catastrophied, constantly under fire,
helpless, abhorred, just a glimpse
of a world pre-wasteland, pre-ending,
an apocalypse birthed upon our mind,
an excruciating freedom, prophesying,
experiencing, everything as it is:

blind, wretched, naked, and poor,
what more can we ask for
here, among the hollow men?

white garments, eye salve, gold refined by fire?
even now we doubt this infi-legitimate offer;
lest our eyes see;
and oh, we glimpse everything exposed;
lest our ears hear
and oh, our hearts finally be known;
lest our souls bow and how we find
the belief we so desperately need;
yes, i do, i will, i can, i agree to
exchange everything, all i see and don't see,
all that's given and still discovering,
for you, this hand knocking, knocking, knocking.

i had a nightmare
and i awoke.
i ran
to the room of my father.
i crawled into bed
and lay next to him.
in the folds of his blankets
with my head on his chest.
his warm breath
and calm presence
soothed me.

i had a nightmare
and the nightmare was our world.

Prelude: Wandering Home

I still feel at home in the rolling hills of the East Bay Area. There's a time, mid-summer, when all the green has been wrung out of the grass, and the hillsides appear to be covered with golden wheat.

When I walk those trails on a quiet evening, the dry heads of grass scrape against each other. Almost whispering. Almost praying.

The warm summer sunset unwraps, exposing the cool shadows of night. The contours of this hillside hide secret places of refuge. Mysterious pockets of evening, where my mind can rest.

Stillness creeps in. This is a place very few stay. Where fewer remain. A place to get so lost one could finally be found.

> Somewhere we know that without a lonely place our lives are in danger.
>
> Somewhere we know that without silence words lose their meaning, that without listening speaking no longer heals, that without distance closeness cannot cure.
>
> Somewhere we know that without a lonely place our actions quickly become empty gestures.
>
> - Henri Nouwen, *Out of Solitude*

Wandering Home

i have found a home
in love's low hills
you'd never notice me,
as you traced over their golden backs.
the waves of reeds sing
quietly muttering "today" and "now,"

and i do not worry about it,
you know, all those dirty things
our minds play games with while we're gone,
no, i am no harlot here,
my home is the earth,
under the sun,
in the dirt,
away from all.

and you are invited
to our home of listening and waiting,
to meet in the Great Silent Song
and rest.

do I sing here?
yes.

i keep my longing in my pocket
and bring it out on rainy days
it reminds me of your
constant presence
and lifts my heaviness away.

and when you see my pocket treasure
how you smile, i know—
because your life
has bought my treasure
and now it's all i own.

Prelude: Broken Wing

At twenty, I found the wrinkled cover and worn yellow pages of *The Pursuit of God* on my family's bookshelf. The book smelled like an old library. Inside was an inscription from one of my Dad's friends,

> I really believe if you read this book and put into practice the things that make for the pursuit of God, your life will explode with joy.

These lines intrigued me, so I turned the page. A.W. Tozer gazed right through me. He reached out, grabbed my collar and, in a gristly 1940's Midatlantic growl, said:

> In this hour of all-but-universal darkness one cheering gleam appears...there are to be found increasing numbers of persons... marked by a growing hunger after God Himself.

> They are eager for spiritual realities and will not be put off with words, nor will they be content with correct "interpretations" of truth.

> They are athirst for God, and they will not be satisfied till they have drunk deep the Fountain of Living Water.

>   - A.W. Tozer, *The Pursuit of God*

Broken Wing

pursue peace broken wing,
open heaven and bring in
draughts of light in amber flagons,
let us sip once again
the nectar that formed us from dust,
breathed in us, and made us men.

sweetness only comes
in the absence of death
(or at least death in context).

oh, Deliverer,
You look upon misery,
even our emblazoned lips,
and spill over with compassion,
You reach an understanding right hand
to the un-royal, the un-embraced;

oh, how You've hidden
treasures deeper and deeper,
the more layers peel back
the closer is the core,
oh, how the senses intensify,
the sweetness bursts in brilliant flavor,
complex and savory, if only, ever only,
in Your arms we rest;
undress our weary skins
and let You unveil
beloved secrets
whispered only to
the beloved.

logs crackle in flame.
i breathe soot in out as
steam wisps like a ghost i sip.

love is such a face that has grown
unfamiliar over the years,
oh it has come close,
but it's just as blurred.
i can't make it out.
so still i go and stay
i play the game,

but love is like shadow,
coming close, just beyond my eyes,
a form i can't make out
and well i see it
and oh i feel it
but can i know it
does it see me here?

LAMENT

Prelude: In the Potter's Field

There is no better therapy than to dwell on betrayal in Scripture. Plus, it's free. Well, it cost Jesus a lot but now it's free.

> Waking alone
> At the hour when we are
> Trembling with tenderness
> Lips that would kiss
> Form prayers to broken stone.

> - T.S. Eliot, *The Hollow Men*

When Judas, his betrayer, saw that Jesus was condemned, he changed his mind and brought back the thirty pieces of silver to the chief priests and the elders, saying, "I have sinned by betraying innocent blood."

They said, "What is that to us? See to it yourself." And throwing down the pieces of silver into the temple, he departed, and he went and hanged himself. But the chief priests, taking the pieces of silver, said, "It is not lawful to put them into the treasury, since it is blood money."

So they took counsel and bought with them the potter's field as a burial place for strangers. Therefore that field has been called the Field of Blood to this day.

> - Matthew 27.3-8

In the Potter's Field

i am sitting in the potter's field
awaiting the price of blood,
i have been sitting oh so long
between the bracken and the shrubs.

so quiet, ever still,
though the earth quakes beneath
and i have been thinking angry thoughts
dwelling on bitter things.

gnawing, always gnawing,
on the inside and the out
my teeth gnash with a thousand thoughts
i wish i could do without.

running fingers over clumps of dirt
they shatter in my grasp,
i remember the breaking bread
and the wine i once was promised.

my hands press down, press down,
pressing into the softened earth,
i know my voice sleeps trapped beneath
the layers of rocks and dirt.

friends i once called strangers
compatriots of bitter war;
i think of flowing tears
and the fragrance of the whore;

all gone, all abandoned,
in the kingdom of myself,
do the mountains ever move here?
as i press my hands toward hell.

quiet now, thin coin bag,
my pocket full of holes,
i retuned you to your grave
i gave you back—leave me alone!

leave me, just leave it,
can't you just leave me on my own?
i've never been so scared,
so unsacred, so enstoned.

leave it, now my spirit,
i remember my mother's words,
i remember my father's eyes;
oh, the blessing and the curse.

i remember the beloved in water
the sky rent wide as wheat
yet here i sit 'mongst the graves
broken, defiled, and weak.

i kissed him, oh, i kissed him,
i kissed him like a whore,
now i sit waiting,
thinking of the blood i have abhorred,
and the blood i still ignore,
ever still, ever soft, quaking beneath this earth,
oh, i do remember, the blessing and the curse.

Lucy leaned her head on the edge of the fighting top and whispered, "Aslan, Aslan, if ever you loved us at all, send us help now." The darkness did not grow any less, but she began to feel a little—a very, very little—better....

There was a tiny speck of light ahead, and while they watched a broad beam of light fell from it upon the ship. Lucy looked along the beam and presently saw something in it....an albatross. It called out in a strong sweet voice what seemed to be words though no one understood them....

No one but Lucy knew that as it circled the mast it had whispered to her, "Courage, dear heart," and the voice, she felt sure, was Aslan's, and with the voice a delicious smell breathed in her face.

- C.S. Lewis,
The Voyage of the Dawn Treader

Prelude: A Vessel Made and Remaking

God is in the business of making things. And He's really, really good at it. Just look around. His specific creative attention is on humanity.

> For the eyes of the Lord move to and fro throughout the earth that He may strongly support those whose heart is completely His.

> *- 2 Chronicles 16.9*

God has already chosen humanity. It's a done deal. And He's willing to form us. The choice to commune and grow is on our side.

> He did so to make known the riches of His glory upon vessels of mercy, which He prepared beforehand for glory, even us.

> *- Romans 9.23*

We are created to be filled with God's presence. Treasure in earthen vessels. Sometimes we need a touch up, bit of sealant, or tender rebuilding. I mean, we're only clay. Jeremiah the prophet saw this as he watched the potter at work.

> Then the word of the Lord came...saying, "Can I not...deal with you as this potter does? Like clay...so are you in My hand."

> *- Jeremiah 18.5-6*

A Vessel Made and Remaking

i went down to the potter's house
and there he was making
some form upon the wheel,
but the vessel spoiled in his hand,

so he gently crushed it
and remade the form to his liking;

can he not deal with me as the potter's pleasure?
bending, breaking, even remaking me
into a thousand forms to suit his measure?

am i not dust and water pressed together
with the breath and effort
of infinite, delicate hands?

behold, my eyes see my form
and with me, millions of vessels
ready to be filled with reward.

do you wish to be beautiful?
what do you long to contain?
where are your edges breaking?
what can bend and be remade?

as the clay is in the hand of the potter
so are we in him this very hour
a vessel made and remaking
for honor.

Prelude: Swing Low

This is another two-part series penned within months of each other. I can't explain why this old-time song, *Swing Low Sweet Chariot,* came to mind, and framed both poems. I recall singing it in playschool as a child and later with hand-motions while counseling at summer camp.

Swing Low Sweet Chariot is an old African American hymn sung during the days of slavery. It recalls the story of Elijah, who after long years of serving God, is swept away in a chariot of fire, leaving his protégé, Elisha, behind to continue the work.

> As they were going along and talking, behold, there appeared a chariot of fire and horses of fire which separated the two of them. And Elijah went up by a whirlwind to heaven.
>
> Elisha saw it and cried out, "My father, my father, the chariots of Israel and its horsemen!" And he saw Elijah no more.
>
> - 2 Kings 2.11-12

A powerful story of deliverance and salvation, it's a reminder of God's invasion into our reality and His ability to bring us ultimate comfort in heaven.

For me, it holds a taste of hope in the struggle to understand our circumstances and a foretaste of our final rest at "home in greater knowns."

Swing Low: Displaced

swing low sweet chariot
comin' forth to carry me home.
swing low sweet chariot
coming forth to carry me home.)

sat still with hope
she waited on me, questioned—
i answered with a wink,
smiled strained happiness
and mentioned her name,
wondered and modeled
(and still wondered just the same).
our wants and answers play a silly game,
like lovers self-aware, unsure, question fate.

swing low,
sweet me away,
chariot of wants
days unclaimed,
come forth,
in majesty unmeasured,
unattained—
and wait to be lifted, upheld
displaced.

meet with me for coffee?

tomorrow?

it's a date.

well sure, unless you're unsure, if so then let's just wait.

but i do, and you?

of course, it's true,

and we court, and flit, and faint.

swing low, deeper song—
melody unclaimed,
resonate
singing full the note always unmade
and want the straight
unending wants
to adore
to exalt
to Remain.

(we worship One forever,
One we worship.
One the same.

Swing Low: Known

swing low
sweet chariot
coming forth
to carry me home
swing low
sweet chariot
coming forth to carry me home.

the flow
the violent flow of quiet unknowns
helps to settle the nerves
and stretch hands
for home in greater knowns.

which find me stripped,
running free inside
revealed in the light of all-knowledge
      pass the gas lights
      the street lamps
      even the storytellers
      straight to the heart of life.
      the majestic sun, the wonder that scars
      and burns and skips rocks across my heart;

      proceed in abandon, unwise decision
      silly and wreak-less notions
      of the human condition
      inside all perfection.
shout all you see, all you know of him—
and swear you'll keep clean
in a better heart; in perfect seeing,

what is hidden? nothing!
so what is imperfect in this love?
nothing will escape
the authors pen,
the artist's touch—
even our escape must be in love.

> and i present myself
> to the will unknown to me
> to the will that's not my own
> to be Yours and Yours completely.

Jesus,
i believe You—even when i don't see,
i believe You because
I know You believe in me.
and though, even now, i feel a little lost,
Jesus, i believe You no matter what the cost

when my heart is dark, and Lord,
i feel deaths lonesome call
i believe You even now, my God
or i don't believe at all…

Prelude: The Shoreline

At the end of another silent retreat I sat by the shoreline and touch my pen to my journal. The words became a lament, a heart expression while God seemed absent. Some theologians consider lament the highest form of worship. Countless psalms engage with God on this level, wrestling with Him about His promises and character and begging Him to come through in their situation. Over half the book of Psalms is lament poetry.

The ancients speak of two categories for our worship experience: consolation, the sense of God's presence near to us, and desolation, the sense of God's presence far from us. This tension creates the ebb and flow of our Christian life. *The Shoreline* is a poem of desolation, a lament lifted to God. It is hard to read, but ripe with significance, for it reveals contours of the heart rarely glimpsed in seasons of consolation.

Why are laments so valued? Because lament engages the entire human being in honest conversation with God. This is worshiping in spirit and in *truth*, our attention is turned to Him, even when it's hard. A truly good Father loves to have His kids close to Him, *especially* while it's hard.

The Shoreline

stretching long
oh, the vastness of all thought—
i am trapped here
and i am scrapping against the rocks.

the well is deep, too deep
too deep to touch the bottom
and i am wading waiting here,
for a sip of some sweet water.

am i a desert wanderer
over sandhills brown and gray?
or am i a seasick sailor
holding out for shore or bay?

how can You leave me so alone here,
so fragile, so expectant?
i thought You'd come home by now
but it's been long, long past sunset.

what is it to hope for You
to be *in* You while You're away?
i cannot find the door or path You took
it's all scattered, all fake.

and i have asked to be examined,
yet it only seems like me;
my own reason is my doctor,
my thought my remedy.

how can You be apart here?
i am still that little boy
whom You dropped off at mother's
and left us unemployed.

i've scattered all my reasons
to the wind above the water
and watched her carry them
away from me forever,

yet i'd hoped you'd find them
and piece them back together
but all i know is seaward
and scattered there, my treasure.

i whisper to the wind
or does she to me?
but we speak a different language
as she carries my thoughts to sea.

i whisper to the shore
and her rhythmic thought-like waves
but i only hear my heartbeat,
my verity, my grave.

This is what lament does; it pours out our pain at the feet of our Creator. If he does not speak, we will not live. This is the crisis.

If he does not re-tell us our story, then we will be lost in a panoply of lesser stories of our own making…In telling our story to God, we open ourselves up to hearing our story retold….

Listening is the backside of lament…. We might even catch a glimpse of something glorious going on—resurrection.

- Scott Holman,
Learning Lament Between the Paws,
Journal of Spiritual Formation & Soul Care

i love you weakness. suffering too.
sense of loneliness
and broken.
find emptiness,
black soot and me,
the sinking fear and stench of shame—
oh misery, i entreat you still,
to have your way with me.
i am blind to beauty, and flavor (but bitter),
ecstasy and elation;
find your cracked and thirsty ground—
and you will find my heaven.

Prelude: **See Through Me**

As a camp counselors, each morning we would gather the kids and sing together at the amphitheater overlooking the creek. And every morning, at about ten, the sunlight would eek through the Redwood forest and grace the edges of the leaves.

One tree hung above the theater, its leaves large as a man's hand: The Big Leaf Maple. In the moist mountain soil The Big Leaf Maple remained a gorgeous green all summer long. But, when the light of the Sun hit those fringes, the beauty was amplified a hundred-fold.

You could see every green vein of clorophylled life, each fiber beamed into almost a golden yellow. The edges shimmered and shown with radiance. Hundreds of maple leaves joined the chorus of heaven.

Ordinarily, these leaves are beautiful, worthy of taking home and being pressed in a book. But, when illuminated, filled, touched, back-lit by the morning Sun—their splendor was breathtaking.

I can still remember their golden faces shining over the camper's songs.

See Through Me

see through me.
like the x-ray machine, looking through my skin
to the dry bones within, see through me.

see through me.
like the windswept waves burst with lighted beads
of sunrays, crashing only to come up again,
see through me.

see through me.
like the child scraping begging for a playing
mother who sweeps into her arms for the
attention so needed,
see through me.

see through me.
like the renegade son who came back with
nothing, begging for a job, stinking and lost,
see through me.

and see through me,
as the dust settles and the world mentions
my name and maims my faith and shows
my bruised face to you and i wonder there,
mixed with all the mirth and laughter,
with the wealth of nations on our shoulders,
and my illegitimate brother pointing to every way
i've been fake, halfhearted and shamed,
Lord Almighty, will you then?

see through me.

i have been changed
by the blood of an animal.

i've found love inside a wound.

i've been thrashed by a stalking lion
and found love inside my lesions.

i have breathed fragrant oil
dripping off the lion's mane.

i've found anger soften by a whisper.
i've found love inside the grave.

Prelude: Pain

Everyone cringed watching Job suffered at the door of death, as he wondered, just like all of us do, "Is God actually in *this?*" This is a key question for all sufferers. The answer is born in our ability to ask this honestly, over and over. Our healing is in that honest search by which we understand, appropriate, and receive that answer, over and over.

Many say time is a healer. And it can be. Though father time remains a stoic, if not neglectful, parent, without love or comfort or connection. Healing and its fruits are not time-oriented, but relation-oriented. Watching a beautiful sunset only impacts us if we are slow down to appreciate the meaning of that moment. Others just drive by. The meaning becomes manifold when shared with another.

It's really our perception that begins healing. Wounds are reinterpreted by our seasons; new circumstances reveal deeper truths, and as we change in relation to our world, so our whole story does too. Growth in relation to God and others corresponds directly to personal healing. Often the answer to our suffering and the healing of a wound, resides in the comfort of another.

Pain

pain is not meant to be secret
but shared like a meal
before death's door,

nor is it meant
to be whispered in secret
like the silence of a whore.

but my pain
has become
an open conversation

a host with whom i walk
into the expanse of my soul,
and traipse through fields of memories
some dry as sand and others
fertile, rich as a whole forest floor;

and i haven't wanted to admit how
the exhortations of old voices
taught me pain and his accompaniment
are then and now sideways friends,

strange, brutal companions
who make war for our hearts,
endure scourging after scourging with us

as our knees buckle
it is pain that cleans the mind,

as our bones ache
it's longing that binds us up,

when our hearts throb
and threaten to burst
as the worst things imagined
force themselves into action
it isn't only our reason, our logic,
our largesse that calms us down,
it is the violent silence
of not-ever-knowing
what is next,
never knowing
and always knowing
you will never ever know
what threatens you
just around the corner,
as knees tremble
and bones ache
and silence calls us
to the one thing that's
too precious for us
to pry open;
our empty
hands.

I have been scarred so deep
By life and cold despair,
And brittle bones were broken
Far beyond repair…
I have toiled for countless years
And ever felt the cost,
I've been burned by this world's cold,
Like leaves beneath the frost.

If mercy falls upon
The broken and the poor,
Dear Father, I will see you,
There on distant shores…

On my knees, I wept at Your feet,
I finally believed, that You still loved me.
Healing hands of God have mercy
on our unclean souls once again,
Jesus Christ, Light of the World,
Burning bright within our hearts,
Here's my heart,
Let it be forever Yours,
Only You can make
Every new day seem so new.

- Five Iron Frenzy,
On Distant Shores

Prelude: Wordless Place, Parts I & II

On her way to the Governor's Inaugural Ball, Ella Wheeler Wilcox noticed a young woman across the aisle, dressed in black. The woman wept. Ella Wheeler sat beside her for a bit, hoping to provide some small comfort.

Ella couldn't forget the moment. It haunted her through all the Governor's festivities. While glimpsing her own face in the mirror, she still saw the face of that widow.[4]

Soon after she penned the now proverbial line, "Laugh and the world laughs with you, weep, and you weep alone." These words became a testament to human experience. Pain can be so isolating.

After reading the full poem, I've never forgotten her words. It ends with these lines:

> There is room in the halls of pleasure
> For a large and lordly train,
> But one by one we must all file on
> Through the narrow aisles of pain.

> - Ella Wheeler Wilcox, *Solitude*

---

[4] https://en.wikipedia.org/wiki/Ella_Wheeler_Wilcox

Part I: Wordless Place

wherever went the wild wind blows
it goes, it goes, it goes, it goes,

and bluster blown, bent so low,
rustling the depths of sin and bone;
to post-mend by wounding,
by reminding, by bleeding out the sour juices
of bitterness and gall,
here we taste the last trouble of man,
the cup of all the world;

we file on, subscribed by tact,
entering on our mother's back;
one by one, lips sip, and taste the whip,
and drip the waste once draught
by whom it's taught—

our fathers, too, sought a better drink,
but winked away by the same things we wink
and think aren't convincing (but we're all itching).

so, we subscribe and find
the bitter drink ours still,
and worse, must we will the cup
and thank the world for what it brings us?
we drink and smile vials of cordial and guile,
all the while the world wonders with us
why we like the taste.

the whole remains bleeding—
but we're healing, inside revealing

a rich thickness of bitter mixed in white,
covering our lips and our spiteful tongue,
isn't this all that we've winked for?
this, this is it? nothing more?
but our lip service? our canker?
and—of course—the poor?
no, no one is the problem anymore;
no one excuse, no one maligned or restored,
no third party, no discussion,
no choice, no matter, no score;

all rote, all science, all bent bending in,
all winks winking, eyes close to blinding,
darkness and his kind, hiding inside,
oh, what can't we find in
minding our own business,
store closed, windows barred,
and we're hoping for some profit?

somewhere between our mess,
we've slipped into an autopilot,
a lavish meaninglessness,
the great excuse, the poison tip,
the antidote? just one word on our lips,
one simple white word whispered,
heard or unheard, gallant and grim,
soft as a white bird,
flirting between the heavens and earth,

but that whip, but that cup,
oh, that rose, and all her thorns she brings us,
what and who and how slip away
into the doldrums of sunlight and rain,

we no longer hear her song,
we no longer lift our cup,
but what seems gone is never gone,
and so, we file on.

                    : :

in the quiet of a hill top,
far from the clip clop
and buzzing of mouths,
the sows find filling munching and crunching
and smiling at him filing on.

he squeezes a cent
clenched between fingers like teeth,
and he listens like he's never heard anything:

a quiet horn blown?
a passing breeze?
a tiny bird?
oh, the optimist sings of better things—

each looks; the hills, the rocks, the trees,
all familiar sings of better things,

but the ocean deep, it keeps, it knows, it groans,
it goes, it goes, it goes, it goes.

Part II: Wordless Place

wordless place again,
ancient agony's quiet rule.
sea waves roll, still chanting
rhythm and song, chanting slow and long,
"lord, take the bitter cup, still."

again, i question, "is this thy will?
are not all things possible for thee?
then why this way lord? and why me?"

many times, before the throne i passed
untouched, unscathed, undone—yet here—
at the little cut, the small blade;

it was not the wound's size that ached
but the place.
soft.
tender.

well bleed then, but bleed out me
all my self-made dissonance, un-crying un-aching;

well take then, but take out pride
and be patient, while i wail and moan inside.
it's only my heart. my love. my time.

oh, your sure voice recommends me still,
"It's only My heart, My love, My time, My will."

i cry out to the living God
in prayer
in prayer
but is he there?

i cry out to the living God
without words
secret, unheard
but is he near?

i cry out the living God
heart soft
eyes wet
but am i met?

i cry out to the living God
and i weep
for i see nothing
but a list of promises given
only to those who truly listen.

while in despair
i cry out to the living God
in prayer
in prayer.

The stalk has been cut, been wounded, to make an opening to receive the graft. No graft without wounding—the laying bare and opening up of the inner life of the tree to receive the stranger branch. It is only through such wounding that access can be obtained to the fellowship of the sap and the growth and the life of the stronger stem...

In the death of the cross Christ was wounded, and in His opened wounds a place prepared where we might be grafted in.... Abide in the wounds of Jesus; there is the place of union, and life, and growth....His flesh was rent that the way might be opened for thy being made one with Him, and having access to all the blessings flowing from His divine nature.

- Andrew Murray, *Abide in Christ*

Prelude: **Weakness**

Weakness can feel uncomfortable, awkward, and unfinished. It's a hard emotion to face. In fact, many of us run from that precious point of surrender until the last moment.

Francis Thompson spoke of God as the "Hound of Heaven," pursuing His heart no matter what:

> Down the nights and down the days;
> I fled Him, down the arches of the years;
> I fled Him, down the labyrinthine ways
> Of my own mind; and in the mist of tears…
> But with unhurrying chase,
> And unperturbèd pace,
> Deliberate speed, majestic instancy,
> They beat—and a Voice beat
> More instant than the Feet.

> - Francis Thomas, *The Hound of Heaven*

The Hound captured Francis. King David was captured too:

> Where can I go from Your Spirit?
> Or where can I flee from Your presence?
> If I ascend to heaven, You are there;
> If I make my bed in Sheol, You are there….
> Even the darkness is not dark to You,
> And the night is as bright as the day.
> Darkness and light are alike to You.

> - Psalm 139.7-8, 12

123

Weakness

like a wounded animal
my tranquil weakness, my lacking
attracts your great love.
my wounds make you hungry
and my small cries and whimpers
move your great love.

i am a small prey, a petty morsel
for your great appetite;
you are a predator of mercy
a hound of affection,
you weigh me up with great hands
able to crush and dissect
and gentle to heal.

i squirm in a mess of my own making,
i struggle to find my way out;
cause even in grace
my heart is aching,
even in love i'm found.

don't whisper to me, don't whisper i say
all those kind words for a child's soft mind,
for i am wiser, wounded, older,
locked in messes i've defined.

i would press hot irons down,
down to seal and disinfect
if only i could hide from You;
my precious predator,
my unrelenting hound of affection.

i begged you, ancient friend, to come
you've shaken hands with so many,
young or old, strong or broken
and you've fixed 'em
  and loved 'em
  and owned 'em.

Prelude: Driftwood Kingdoms

There's something majestic in the moment just after sunset, something somber, still, and eternal. Standing before that calm glow, the soft waves, the stalwart sands, the driftwood scattered below, I pulled out my pen and words stirred.

At the end of Solomon's reign in Israel, at the height of his kingdom, he surprisingly struggled with grief.

> [God] has…set eternity in their heart, yet so that man will not find out the work which God has done from the beginning even to the end.
>
> - Ecclesiastes 3.11

Meaninglessness can be a gift or a bane. Context matters. Complete meaningless is torture. But in God's story, meaninglessness begins the pangs of repentance, a nudge toward surrender.

> Creation was subjected to futility, not willingly, but because of Him who subjected it, in hope that the creation itself also will be set free.
>
> - Romans 8.20

Meaninglessness beckons rebuilding, renewing, refilling. Taking a step of trust into a better covenant with better promises.

Driftwood Kingdoms

sometimes night falls when you least expect
as the clouds roll in
hiding sunset

and all you can do is sit and sip on
all the things you've left undone,
and the waves that might have come
carrying driftwood kingdoms
to begging hands.

and just so, the sunset darkens before your eyes
but beauty only ashes tithe
which sweeping breezes blow away
toward vast and vacant skies.

as slowly, slowly,
ever so slow
life begins to bleed
into the lies we've been living in,

our little hovels
how they hold us
dull and lifeless,
away from love and kissing lips
away from pain and betrayer's kiss;

and here i sit in darkest night
contemplating what might have been
and why, what i thought might be, isn't.

"no."
it echoes over silhouettes
and pierces me
with a touch of meaninglessness,

hoping for a hand to hold in the shade
but it only seems to grow darker these days.

Now I'm glad—not that you were upset, but that you were jarred into turning things around. You let the distress bring you to God, not drive you from him. The result was all gain, no loss.

Distress that drives us to God does that. It turns us around. It gets us back in the way of salvation. We never regret that kind of pain. But those who let distress drive them away from God are full of regrets, end up on a deathbed of regrets.

And now, isn't it wonderful all the ways in which this distress has goaded you closer to God? You're more alive, more concerned, more sensitive, more reverent, more human, more passionate, more responsible. Looked at from any angle, you've come out of this with purity of heart.

-2 Corinthians 7.9-11, MSG

as the late evening fog sweeps in over the hills
and the cold air creeps
to all the doors and windows,
as the blankets cover and wrap the restful
and the air settles softly among the bedfolds,
as the souls breathe,
and the nostrils rhythm beats
and the warmth of the lungs fills the ventricles—
may the very air sing and pulse and speak
of our Savior who aches to be known.

WONDER

Prelude: A Whisper of These Words

Our histories stay with us. A generation before mine spoke often of character—the capacity to fulfill duty. Current generations struggle to pair duty with desire. There's a constant game going on between childhood wants and adult responsibility: Peter Pan and Captain Hook.

> Peter. I swear to you wherever you go... I vow there will always be daggers buried in notes signed James Hook. They will be flung into doors of your children's children's children, do you hear me?

> \- Captain Hook, *Hook*

Our responsibility can slay or sustain our desires; our desires can develop or disown our duty. But there's only one relationship where no matter how grown up we are, we can always remain a child at heart.

> Well, whoever you are it's still you, 'cause only one person has that smell...of someone who has ridden the back of the wind, Peter...of a hundred fun summers, with sleeping in trees and adventures with Indians and Pirates. Oh remember, Peter? The world was ours. We could do everything or nothing. All it had to be was anything 'cause it was always us.

> \- Tinkerbell, *Hook*

A Whisper of These Words

The color of burntblue,
there on a sunday's eve
clear skies, murky water,
like the leftovers of a childhood memory;
waveuponwave, an endless rhythm beats
like brave drums deep beneath
the twilight heaven.

i'm swinging to and fro,
softer than a leaf resting on the breeze
as weight of the world is lifted
and taken far away from me—

but still remains this pain
holding a raw and bitter heart,
what questions told not to ask anymore
but still feel their beat in the dark.

when you caught me, i don't know,
and when did i realized i'm not alone?
and where will we go from here
when you lift this veil of pain?
i really can't imagine it gone
and me still remain.

swift comes the morning and eve'
oh, something's left behind,
and i have searched the earth in her age
only to long and pine,

for what? i cannot place it,
a face, a friend i never knew?
dream of a dream i once had as a child,
never forgotten, never renewed?

were i to lift it up,
like a rock upon the earth,
what would i find beneath?
grubs, worms, and dirt?
oh, what ugliness, oh, my heart—
oh, how i didn't want to see:

the very knife that is my wound
pierces me for the healing,

water and blood flow out
from where i still know not
and i am bleeding still,
though whose blood i've forgot.

Prelude: Beyond the Edge of the World

Mystery is a terrifying and breathtaking adventure. Western culture works hard to sanitize the unknown, the unpredictable, the out-of-control. As a result, we live in anxious anticipation of life coming undone in a single moment. Even our language hides from the mysterious.

> The word *definition* literally means "of the finite." We define things by virtue of their limitations. To be defined, anything must be small enough to wrap words around it and distinguish it from other things. The question arises, how do you define God?

> - Jerry Root & Mark Neal,
> *The Surprising Imagination of C.S. Lewis*

Any exploration into the heart of God is both an adventure into the unknown and a critique of the known. To engage faith, we build from the rational to relational. Those walls that confined become invitations to discover new depths. Let's stop protecting our walls and find ourselves lost again in the endless heart of God.

> Men suffer much more from imagining too little than too much.

> - P.T. Barnum, *The Greatest Showman*

Beyond the Edge of the World

i have been seeking things beyond the city,
unto the edge of the world,
and though i did not sail there
i saw the edge unfurled.

the cascades endless drop
silent but for downrush sounds
as desperate droplets race higher
and settle in a starlit sky.

and i grew afraid, here,
in this stark unfeeling end;
i'd hoped for faces to look my way
but everything remained still, silent.

dare i ask, "where were the brave,
here at the end of the world?"
the adventures, stragglers, and sojourners,
haven't they too yearned for this fearless place?

and what of the edge,
where the starry host peak over this horizon,
do they alone know the height and depth,
and must i ask to find them?

oh, tell me falls of endless light—
where do your waters meet with land,
and is it peaceful, is it safe,
is it worth this momentous, unfurled end?

and how can i imagine such impossibilities,
won't they always lead away,
from my familiar city, my warm bed,
from my love's precious gaze?

come to me, ends of the earth
that i might learn my end,
but meet me in the city,
and touch the living dead.

i thought i might gain from you
by seeing through your eyes,
but i am finding contentment here
just being seen by Thine.

"If we truly want to follow God, we must seek to be otherworldly."

- A.W. Tozer, *The Pursuit of God*

Prelude: **Among Them**

It's said of Jesus,

> The Light shines in the darkness, and the darkness did not comprehend it…. The world was made through Him, and the world did not know Him.

> - John 1.5, 10

What must this have been like? To live unknown in the world you made? It seems a burden beyond comprehension to truly see, to truly understand, to grasp *aletheia*—which means *reality*. No wonder they called him the "Man of Sorrows."

> For you weigh men down with burdens hard to bear, while you yourselves will not even touch the burdens with one of your fingers.

> For you have taken away the key of knowledge; you yourselves did not enter, and you hindered those who were entering."

> - Luke 11.46, 52

His eyes watched the dismantling of the created order. He comprehended how law and grace could lead everyone to the Father. He knew what was available. He made it available. Even today, we still struggle to comprehend this.

Among Them

among the dark things
came another sounding like them

looking about
searching everywhere
till every corner heard about it

and all came stammering over
in collective voices
to give their two cents
and to see who was commended,

yet in every word,
in every proposal,
in every breathy second
did they ever really know him
or stop to ask him about it?

when the world sings
it seems like everything's in question—

but one nod
a smirk
a tiny suggestion from him and all is stopped—
and the world itself is put into question

for the answer is rhetorical,
obvious, unmentioned.

Jesus was sitting in Moses' chair
They brought the trembling woman there.
Moses command she be ston'd to death.
What was the sound of Jesus' breath?
He laid His hand on Moses' law;
The ancient Heavens, in silent awe,
Writ with cruses from pole to pole,
All away began to roll...
Thou art good, and Thou alone
Nor may the sinner cast the stone.
To be good only, is to be
A God or else a Pharisee.

- William Blake,
The Everlasting Gospel

Prelude: Tombs

> For you are like concealed tombs, and the
> people who walk over them are unaware of it.

> - Luke 11.44

Concealed tombs. What a potent image. Walking
dead, hidden in human skin. This is what Jesus saw
in the hearts and actions of the Pharisees.

In the Torah, if someone walked over a tomb or
touched the dead they were ceremonially unclean.
Unclean means unholy—no longer able to enter
into God's presence or relationship with His
community.

God required the unclean to present sacrifices and
rites in the temple to restore their relationship with
God. Death was a disease that infected the spiritual
life of the whole community.

> For if the sprinkling of [ceremonially] defiled
> persons with the blood of goats and bulls…is
> sufficient for the cleansing of the body, how
> much more will the blood of Christ, who
> through the eternal Spirit willingly offered
> Himself unblemished to God, cleanse your
> conscience from dead works and lifeless
> observances to serve the ever living God?

> -Hebrews 9.13 AMP

Tombs

take a breath
and let the cool of night
settle in on your neck
and come out renewed.

when the variant tombs open case
and the dry death of empty ribcages
splay with ancient breath,

children of anger call on your name
while in their catacombs,
somewhere beneath those graves,
shaking chains keep shaking, shaking,

can you hear volatile and virile?
can you hear reticent and reptile?
oh, the very things that make men ache
the very things that push him to the edge,

what is it really that the world
worries about at night?

when quiet sets in
and the earth slows down—

we know, we know, somewhere deep and low
dead things have made their home in our souls,

and we shake and moan,
we hide and groan;
for we are scared of ourselves.

breath of soul in You
open soul wide as a field
empty as a forest.
i am unincorporated
i am not for sale.

demon arm reaches through
pushing to-do's
and don't-do's
into an unending maze,

but i breath
breath of soul in You
and let those paths fade.

Prelude: Blood and Song

In early 2000's, John Mark McMillan's best friend died in a car accident. His last prayer?

> "I'd give my life today if it would shake the youth of the nation."

McMillan went on to write one of the most powerful youth anthems of the decade—a fulfillment of his best friend's dream.

> He is jealous for me,
> Love's like a hurricane, I am a tree,
> Bending beneath
> The weight of His wind and mercy.
> When all of a sudden, I am unaware
> Of these afflictions eclipsed by glory,
> And I realize just how beautiful You are,
> And how great Your affections are for me.
> Oh, how He loves us.

> - John Mark McMillian, *How He Loves*

McMillian later commented on this song about his friend,

> I sat down to have a dialogue with God and, really, He ended up having a dialogue with me. It's like He was speaking to me through the song.

> - John Mark McMillian, *Relevant Magazine*

Blood and Song

it was a small song
written in blood and timelessness.
it sang beyond itself
and sent ripples over years
to those whose ears
yearned for the hearing.

and, in doing so,
you've dipped me in wisdom
like candle wax,
i am sealed secure
waiting for a match
so i might burn forever—

calming me with words
meant only for me
yet stretching out
to the very sanctuary of time,
where many like me sit and sip and pine
for forever in a moment by moment day;

until in the brilliance of light
wave after wave they come
as a vast, unfinished army
asking for robes and
white clothing;

we stand on a precipice
waiting for a voice to call us onward
yet the distance is ever too far
for us to cover;

so we wait,
for a face we've never seen
to meet us eye to eye
and thank us for a work
we never performed
and carry us
in youthful flight
into the light of early morn,
rising like bright wings in the west.

and i, still in time (a little box, a daily rhyme),
think on this and am blessed
learning of a song rippling over mine,
and inside, and better yet,
a touch of life
like my desires set aflame with light
(rather than the robbing darkness
in which they live this night),

and in some whispered moment
a transport of utter mystery
carries me away

to shine on me just a shadow
of the mirror-lighted face
i will one day see in life,

and kiss the feet of You
who wash daily mine
and celebrate that Love itself
has conquered me through
blood and song.

Prelude: YHWH, my Father

Many find it hard to understand God the Father in the Old Testament. While taking an Old Testament Survey course, I penned these five poems about Him. The contours, conflicts, and seeming contradictions of Israel's history display a Father that is involved, invested, and infinite in power and love.

> The Lord, the Lord God, compassionate and gracious, slow to anger, and abounding in lovingkindness and truth.
>
> - Exodus 34.6

> For the Lord your God is a consuming fire, a jealous God.
>
> - Deuteronomy 4.24

> Let him who boasts boast of this, that he understands and knows Me, that I am the Lord.
>
> - Jeremiah 9.23-24

> Every one who thirsts, come to the waters.... Come, buy wine and milk without money and without cost. Listen carefully to Me, and eat what is good, and delight yourself in abundance. Listen, that you may live.
>
> - Isaiah 55.1-3

I. YHWH, my Father

the ancients sang against
gods made of hands,
taking trees,
shaping rock,
to build then bow to them;

but now our gods are made of mind,
of self and shifting sands,
enlightenment philosophy,
death and armageddons;

i don't know the gods i've made
so practical i'm blind,
but i know you see the god-like-me
i've made of my own mind.

harlotry, though subtler,
drifts inward with the law
and writ upon our hearts is grace
along with rebel flaws;

do we engender our own selves
to follow demons in disguise,
or must we wait and answer You
who sees through all our lies?

many men have writ of this
yet all are blind like me—
unless the tender Spirit lays
upon our vile harlotry

and presses us against Your Love,
Your Power, Wisdom, Grace
unless we answer "yes" to You
in every little way.

it's not our problem, You answer us
to examine, root, and tend,
it's only ours to surrender
to Your uprooting hand,

and let the face of Jesus be our harlotry demand,
the husband of our youth
He calls again and again

when the voices all around
still and cease from His—
how worthy, how worthy, Lord
to receive honor, praise, and this:

our attention, Jesus
my attention, affection, adoring love—
until all of me is wrought in You
my image, my Lord, my God.

II. YHWH, my Father

when shall i see Your face?
when will i look You in the eye?
certainly, i have fled so many times
(You know i cannot hide).

words will not be enough
the twisting Spirit freely gives
thoughts that pour my spirit through a sieve,

oh, dearest, let my motion be among
those who've served You deep and long.

if we hold our fleeting hearts,
bring love back again.
if we wait among the crowd,
let Your voice speak within.
when the silly questions enter,
how tenderly You understand.

yes do, let's, be, hold, when, oh, dearest, when?

i sit before Your throne,
and did i wander here?
i sit before You asking
and thinking ear to ear,

"whom do i have but You?
and who do i desire like You?
my heart and flesh may fail,
but You are enough
always enough."

III. YHWH, my Father

tenderly
You answer every need You make for me,
i, in turn, sing to You and worship
in Your freedom.

can the world see You
in the messes in the shards?
yet i have cast all things off
to know You as You are.

turning until, again, my stalled heart has raced
filled with motion, motion stalling motion
in this stillness, in this space,
the movements cease to be just movement;
the moments cease to be just a moment—

now so much more,

letting You in, letting all You mean to me,
be filled with all You mean to You—

and still truth cannot quench love,
nor can death separate truth,
nor can one and one ever again make two,
only one now, only

You me You.

IV. YHWH, my Father

let the world lead me out beyond
the stretch of time to timelessness—
looking over a round horizon
the very earth is a blur
between thousands of unimagineds and redefines;

and when, oh when, can i be with You?
oh, of all things, the Maker,
oh, of all things, the very center,
the high, wide, deep and oh so longing for You
in me, letting all this be...

let it be.

You have boundless energy,
as i peer over the fence—people upon people
talk, click, move, wait, question,
complain, forgive, wonder, anger,
laugh, hurt, find and listen,

when can i be *withYou*, YHWH,
there in the silent cosmos,
in the brightening daylight,
in the moving crowds of dimly burning wicks
smoldering in a sunset of Your presence—i am
fine, here...

in my house, in the kitchen,
writing on a table,
looking at a world that's

more or less like me—
and do i see or listen or wait?
do i talk, move, wonder, complain?
do i mutter, mumble, laugh, or pray?

withYou i am beyond question,
i am within resurrection;
unbounded, unlimited,
unhestitating, undone.

V. YHWH, my Father

o taste and see that YHWH is good
He comes to those who fear Him
and rescues them;
He is near to those who seek Him
His ways are beyond the soul, the eyes,
He's bidden us to come find Him
in all the vast avenues of life.

when the soul has journeyed beyond the edge,
that cliff edge of understanding—
and walked that downward path
to the crevices of weakness winding,
winding down into the hole without a crown.

what has been carved over millenniums
in the gorge between life and death?
what hand has shaped the path
spiraling into to emptiness?
reason turns its nose
from the litter and decaying;
faith shields her eyes
from the vulgar still displaying;
the body cringes, repulsed, reflexing within;
what has happened to the soul
in all its beauty, all its innocence?

rivers and streams once her bounty,
mountains, hills, and valleys low,
lands, and oceans, kingdoms, skies,
every meadow, every knoll

once then, and now, is tugging
the heart like a child's hand
but this isn't a world for children anymore, no,
these are the valleys of desolation
rank with bodies of indiscretion;
secrets locked down deep
rotting like a corpse secret souls keep
and never, ever open up;

heirlooms of ancestry,
walls and wounds of blood;
the friends of our community
carrying chains and chains of judgment;
the barrels of our wrath and spite
broken, spilt on the sands,
as wild animals feast on feces
our only hope, our only nourishment;

and with me, all the world,
swallows hard the heavy lump
violated by our violation
festering still in our seven stomachs;

and we attempt to sing, to whistle,
to whisper hope in the void below
somewhere far above the songbird flies
as we grasp for a second note;

we fight but courage dies
torn to pieces by wolves of rote.
and i ask you here, where is He, where,
that good Father of which we once spoke?

can you even find one shred of evidence
of souls dressed, encloaked in linens,
given freely from a wounded hand
forever ever open?

i don't know 'bout you but i'm gunna find
where blood, honey, and leaven mix
to bake bread, mull wine,
and brew spirits strong enough
to lift us from internal armageddon;

where open wounds speak soothing words
and affection breaks attention to infection,
drawing our ear, our eye, our mind
into a lovely open vision,

fresh water bubbles up
from deeper wells, deeper still
than the ones jacob built or moses spilt
through heartrocks hardened fast,

the hallways of our hearts open to a vast,
vast love, come here, come now, come on
horses and chariots with thousands
upon thousands who bow and run all at once,
to the voice whose beckon restores innocence
with love-filled, tender consequences
fit for my good, fit for a king
carrying a son on his shoulders

love touching unlovely, lifting affection,
effecting soil into a life of resurrection,
watered with oil, nourished with light,
bursting into an army brilliant and white
cleaning, cleansing, working, building,
remaking all that's wrong into right, right now.

and i won't blame you, if you bow out here,
'too good to be true' is the sign of a wounded ear
as the gavel, the sword, the hand, and the wound,
work as one to rebuild, rejoice, renew;

as the soul's rift becomes a landing strip
for the decent of grace in the face of our Father-
in-skin always facing facing 'n kindly remakin' us,
every bruise, every crevice, everything,
the soul learns again to speak, to own, to fly
higher and higher as the gaze of her Father
honors her again with mounts and fields,
rivers, lakes, and oceans,

all blowing, bowing, roaring and clapping
in her honor, the honor of honors,
to be restored in love,
to be made again in the gaze of God,

with that smile He wraps a thousand generations
in a word spoke by Three and touching every one
in one little act of faith, we (and our world)
are released in hope, bled in love,
found and planted, entwined forever
in this never, ever ending affection,
our beginning, middle, and end.

Prelude: **Dawn has Come**

On the last day of our backpacking trip, my friends and I descended into a tattered pine forest, where hundreds of trees lay flat as sheaves. Patches of blue sky reached through the green canopy. Standing trunks gazed upon on their fallen comrades. The devastation was immense and unusual, like some storybook giant rampaged through leaving a shattered forest in its wake. Sharp pine fragrance rose from the floor.

There was something miraculous in those fallen woods, so destructive and still so beautiful.

> The God of glory thunders...
> The voice of the Lord is powerful,
> The voice of the Lord is majestic.
> The voice of the Lord breaks the cedars;
> Yes, the Lord breaks in pieces the cedars...
> The voice of the Lord shakes the
> wilderness...and strips the forests bare;
> And in His temple everything says, "Glory!"

> - Psalm 29.3-9

God's raw power. Maybe the Psalmist glimpsed something like I did in this pine forest? In a word God tears down mountains, opens the earth, and in another he whispers and rebuilds our hearts.

Dawn has Come

twirling down
and settling below the crown and face
i stayed thinking only of what had been
and how i could keep it;

yet, one word,
one little word from you
and the trees fell
the oaks bent
the world ceases in motion
(a momentous clearing, rough as dust settles
as if the forest ripped open into naked blue).

and i was so aware ofeverythingalltogether
bowed low by a (whisper) spoken through.

and too, i felt naked
hiding behind anything i could find,
scurrying from log to limb to rock and bush,
from the voice that came and beckoned
with uprooting questions:
(the kind in which both parties
already know the answer).

and i laugh now that it's all over
but then and still the answer shakes me,
and i am seen through,
though the darkness overtakes me,
and haven't yet found myself
in the messesmaking;
but the dontleavemehere

and the imalreadytaken, compoundedtogether,
bridging the words of now-into-forever,
over-the-bend to then,
still dabbling in the maybe,
who knows, and certainly
these things will come to be;

caught here in the forest laid low
where sky bears down, dust settles,
and the glow up-rises in me,
springing not in force, no, but blooming
like a flower at the proper hour
bears its rose,

and all is lifted from the hiding places
and all our faces break into tears and smiles
and embraces:

to those hidden with me
sheltered 'mongst the shrubs
see that you've been seen,
and rest easy, dawn has come.

take me, Jesus, to the place where You
demur from man, take my hand
and bend me low
as the rocks that cry,
as the sparrow dies
so satisfied,
unworried with who You are;
the breath the breathless know far better.

demur: \dih-**mur**\ n. — *the act or an*
instance of objecting: protest[5]

---

[5] https://www.merriam-webster.com/dictionary/demur

Prelude: Sometimes

> This is the day that the Lord has made; let us rejoice and be glad in it.
>
> - Psalm 118.24

Some people spring out of bed with a smile on their face, but the practice of rejoicing has been a struggle for me. Don't get me wrong, I love smiling and I enjoy joy. But over the years, mornings have sometimes been a battle, a canvas where the drama of my relationship with God is played out in real time. He's always near, but it can be a war to fully access this perspective. Psychology provides a helpful concept called *resistance*.

> [Resistance] is used to describe the direct or indirect opposition of a patient to the therapeutic process.[6]
>
> - PsychCentral.com[1]

Resistance can be present in our times with God. We can spend minutes, hours, days, even years, wrestling with Him. In this inner drama, we must dialogue into surrender, lay our anxieties down, then we can experience His peace. This is the heart-work of faith.

---

[6] https://psychcentral.com/encyclopedia/resistance/

Sometimes

sometimes it's overwhelming to think
of this incomprehensible thing
i'm swept up in.
and sometimes all i want
is to bury my face in your cloak—
just to be close;
to lay my head on your chest
as we stare at the clouds and the sky.

sometimes worry holds my day like the reaper,
ready to seize her in the purity of morning;
this ancient law of men, this medieval practice,
a passive release to the ruler of my life,
who scars and pains my first moments.

i am a jealous and passive lover.

: :

sometimes i wish to take the rays of the sun
and swing on them like tarzan,
a boyhood dream: to climb them
without burning my hands,
so much effort to get such a bright thing;
instead i lay on the grass
and let them pierce my epidermis.

sometimes, when the day is gone, i mourn her—
for i never got to say, "hello,"
and she's too unfamiliar now to say, "goodbye;"
this sense of insecurity

keeps me from pursuing her
and wooing her;
to tell her of her beauty,
and truly how much she means to me.

imagine instead, myself with confidence,
a strong forearm pressed against
the small of her back,
my fingers brush away her hair
and our hearts pulse there in that moment.

but, oh God, to what end?
today, i die, the day silks,
and i, like slime, sputter and dry
in the gutter of my own mind;
she, like lavender and fragrance of rose,
and i, like the ashes that merrily repose.

sitting still, my legs swing,
my feet click as they hit,
can a child be with such an ancient lover?
she will pass me and pat me on the head
and say, "how adorable, you in your suit."
that piercing smile, she meant to be sweet;
oh, how i hate it.

"dearly beloved" matters nothing here,
i am a deer and she the huntress,
this backwards death: the piercing arrow,
and the blood: my flowing sorrow;
in her hand the knife that guts me,
and my skin she wears as a final mocking.

oh that day, that year that time is stopping;
on that day, my love, my final mocking.

i am a jealous lover so, i live the jealous lover's woe.

: :

sometimes i sit with my head in my hands
and remember that love is backwards,
and beckons, always backwards,
settling beyond the end of days;
this fragrance of a different time,
of wood, earth, of sawdust and shavings.

finally, a place where i my suit forsake,
as if her womb travailed already,
the day is a mere servant here, and i am a son.

the pulse of infatuation calms
and a strong arm surrounds
and speaks, "peace! be still!"
as a great song arose-in-my-soul,
and beat deeper than love can go.

i am a lover still, but love i know.

: :

sometimes i gather all my moments in the fire
and burn them to know you now.

sometimes i gather all my moments in the fire
and burn them to know you now.

"Surely this youth will not serve our ends," said I, "for he weeps."

The old woman smiled. "Past tears are present strength," said she.

"Wait a while," said the woman; "if I mistake not, he will make you weep till your tears are dry forever. Tears are the only cure for weeping. And you may have need of the cure, before you go forth to face the giants."

- George MacDonald, *Phantastes*

Prelude: The Insufficiency of Words

> Unless your faith is firm, I cannot make you stand firm.
>
> - Isaiah 7.9

Relationships are dynamic, especially divine ones, it's God who invites us into a wrestling match. The push and pull. The explained and unexplainable. The response and responsibility. Who initiates? Who is to blame? How much do I actually contribute? Everyone gets a chance to walk with God. But some seem to walk closer.

> Enoch walked [in habitual fellowship] with God [in reverent fear and obedience]; and he was not [found among men], because God took him [away to be home with Him].
>
> - Gen 5.24 *AMP*

> Without faith it is impossible to please Him, for he who comes to God must believe that He is and that He is a rewarder of those who seek Him.
>
> - Hebrews 11.6

Maybe there's a place for effort in faith? Sometimes it's called *seeking*. Often the gift of faith can be found in that secret place, slowly unwrapped and then treasured forever.

The Insufficiency of Words

i am jacob's child and intend to keep it that way;
inside the fallen, reason and faith propagate
an ancient battle of words and faith;

i pray and forget, or better yet,
i practice forgetfulness on a circuit track;
all light and matter, all hope and hereafter,
is in the recall, the remembrance,
the altered origin, the resemblance,
the source severed or savored,
separated or conjugated,
divorced, ingested,
from the endless sigh of God;

we long for a history bright, that fits our ache,
if only we could remember our own name;
and for the nameless, aching is all the same,
all nature veiled behind vanity and shame;

so pray i forget this,
and pray hard, dear brother,
for our minds have known
more than we've intended;

the future, a sanctuary
where dreams spatter
at father fear's feet;
we are much more religious
than we'd like to believe.

take me, please, to (that wordless place)
the pen i cannot escape,
this stone heart chiseled, carved, engraved,
fingerprints verified: ancient as the Face.

are you like me, so, so tired of
putting meaning on meaning things?

definition is its own burden;
we write our own graves
and wonder why
our souls waste away?

(wait)

just. wait. seriously, wait a minute here with me.

are we just pushed along
or pulled between,
with many men musing a little,
noting e'ry lil' jot and tittle
of what is and has always been,
drawing lines between our lesions?
oh, where are the ancients when they are needed?
and why, why, why are we so interested?
it's *just* existing.

no big deal.
breathe.
laugh.
smile.

"hey, come on, why still unsettled?"

(but these questions beg to be asked,
practically scraping as metal against glass,
the faceless face, of the homeless alone,
the addict, the pornographer,
the hypocrite, the controlled,
it's practically habit now—
but social cues never say that somehow)

just wrench it down, deep down,
far, far beneath coinvent words,
chosen to keep the chosen in;
even outcasts protect their prejudices:
our fingers a pen,
our fist a sign,
our palm a paper,
our faces a rhyme,
our figures a fire,
our feet to bind,
tis only and ever
the blind leading the blind.

while somewhere far away,
a voiceless voice screams in pain,
raking nails on a chalkboard,
piercing, wailing in vain;

we plug our ears and shut it out,
and clench our teeth like a fist,
until it's barely a sound
so intrinsic
you'll swear never even existed,

butit'sjustcrowdedoverhere
inthiscornerandit'sclaustroph
obicblurtingobscenitiesbeca
useitreallycan'tcontrolanythi
ngit'sfeelinganymoreandally
ourdoingispushingitmoreand
moretowardstheedge

till one day,
on an ordinary morning,
everyone arrives nominal as usual,
with coffee cups and
forgotten-to-brush-in-a-rush teeth
stained yellow from the drink
(or bleached porcelain-white as a sink),

'bout mid-afternoon you realize
Hal never showed
as you glance at his desk
he kicks the doors,
lifts an AK-47, and with a grimace
shoots everyone who ever
smirked at him.

there's some unnerved tension
at that oncoming thought,
how suddenly he went
from "genuinely good person"
to "hell bent and wicked,"
we are all baptist preachers
if the moment asks for it,
it's just profits and losses,
kingdoms and crosses.

and we think we really know those around us?
the barista, the clerk, the lawyer, the defendant?
we spin and speak of politics
in some residential limerick
(that found us on the internet
and now is shaping
our very thought and decision),

the ancients seemed to get it,
"but things are somuchmore complicated,"
it almost says itself, this mental chore,
accusing instead of cleaning our moral mores,
"impossible" is the word of choice,
passive is the new active voice—
maybe we're just further from the Source?

in this survival of the fittest,
we claw our way to transcendence
a self-prescribed division, (it's science),
growth based on violence;
in due course, if one really did get better,
here among the islands of neutral,
we would only die alone,
in the boat of our own starving souls,
a slow prophetic exile, mile upon mile.

dangerous, dangerous is goodness,
and any notion of perfection
gets under the skin
changes hope,
changes action;

"careful with the questions,
they cause the mind to play games,"
(though such games are rarely played nowadays);

"it's all a matter of perspective," they say,
"read a book, take a quiz,
hear podcast, find a date,
it's all relative—anything just find your place,
that special place where you are you,"
but that isn't so helpful if your dying for truth,
if your dying for a comforting word,
something to sooth, to bring heaven to earth.

but isn't that the funny thing about words?
they burn and then fade like smoke in your lungs
dirtied not by what comes in but what comes out
(or doesn't).

words hide and heckle in a providential residence;
they slip and slide like a psychedelic experience;
they tremble and crumble in the aches of despair;
they color the truth until it's barely there;
they flit and faint and hide among the bedfolds;
they crush n' gage, til you "do what you're told,"
they laugh and play until neglect is naught;
they hold in their hand the silence they forgot;
they forget the word unheard before their name;
they forget and in their forgetting
all they speak is the same;

it's words that make our violent verbs move;
and power the nouns to label and prove,
the adjectives, delicate, destined, distinct;

easily rebrewing the blood in their instincts;

dirtied now like a mouthful of regret;
dirty words we can never forget;
words making mockery of the Maker's song,
words polluting all our mouth and lungs;
from the throat of the sinner
to the throat of the saint,
dirty little words rot
like an open grave.

(many once pointed hands fall;
as a voice echoes against the walls
of our hearts hardened fast,
listening first, speaking last.)

can you find the whispersong
beneath those words?
syntax burns in the mouth,
while the cry of the kidneys, the gut, eeks out;
the cry of the infant babbling for more,
the stories of family, faith, and folk-lore,
marked by both mary's: virgin and whore;
words rising from words never spoken before,
words from the word
before words were enworded;
words of earth and angels in worship;
words of the Spirit speaking over the earth
that forgotten word spoken long before the curse.

silence.

somewhere between violence and violence,
rises the fragrant moment
of you and me
stuck inside
a word of three.

allow it to sneak in,
to come to fruition,
and you will find
the greatest wrestling match
mankind was ever given.

that day that jacob became israel,
what ends to him we owe;
the moan of michelangelo;
the epiphanies of thoreau;
what rote, what song,
what quaint pirouette,
can lay claim or boast of this?

that he who hath wrestled with God,
is he that will endureth.

oh love, your love, it tastes like bread;
it feels like tears;
it drips and drips
patient drops round
as hazelnuts, real as
blood, tight as flesh,
strong as timelessness,
innocent as childhood,
pure and ignorant, this
is the love you love with;
it is all, just this.

And in this God showed me something small, no bigger than a hazelnut, lying in the palm of my hand. It seemed to me as round as a ball. I gazed at it and thought, 'What can this be?'

The answer came thus, 'It is everything that is made.'

I marveled how this could be, for it was so small it seemed it might fall suddenly into nothingness.

Then I heard the answer, 'It lasts, and ever shall last, because God loves it. All things have their being in this way by the grace of God.'

- Julian of Norwich,
Revelations of Divine Love

Prelude: There is a Song Between Two Persons

> What was from the beginning, what we have
> heard, what we have seen with our eyes, what
> we have looked at and we have touched with
> our hands, concerning the Word of life—has
> been made manifest.

> - 1 John 1. 1-3

The kingdom of God is real, not just real, but real-time, not just real-time, but written into every atom and molecule of the created order. God spoke "very good;" all the universe trembles still.

> This is my father's world
> And to my listening ears
> All nature sings, and round me rings
> The music of the spheres.

> - Maltbie D. Batcock,
> *This is My Father's World*

Every corner of the universe beckons prayer, if only we would look for it. From our breath to our bodies, our spirits to our souls, God made every facet of the human being for Himself.

> There are no unsacred places; there are only
> sacred places and desecrated places.

> - Wendell Berry, *How t*
> *Be a Poet*

There is a Song Between Two Persons

i bow to you, God omnipotent;
i reach for you, God omnipresent;

i look for you, God all-wise;
i hope for you, God all-good;

i sing for you, God creator;
i dance for you, unmoved mover.

i breath for you, ever-present;
i stop for you, eternal moment;

i rest on you, sure foundation;
i let go for you, i let go.

"I am powerful over you, bow;
I am present over you, reach;

I am considerate over you, look;
I am good over you, hope;

I am making over you, sing;
I am moving over you, dance;

I am present over you, breathe;
I am over you, cease;

I am confident in you, rest;
I am, my son, I am."

the birds soaring, my soul in You.
the clouds moving and forming, my heart.

the blue is blue because of You,
and night arrives when You hide.

the greens, the life i have in You.
the reds, the works You have done.

the life around me and in me is You,
i am in You; we are one.

the stars, i know them as glimmers of You.
the sun, Your hope in my heart.

the twigs, the moments i break for You.
the seasons, my soul in Your art.

the questions, the mind i have for You.
the hurts, Your way in my way.

the branches, all that i stretch toward you.
am i not the world You have made?

"son, when i made the stars and the sun,
you were a thought in My mind.

when I touched the earth and caused it to grow
I pressed myself in your eyes.

when I set the clock to tick quiet joy
I wound your heart around Mine.

just try and you'll find, low and high,
e'ry place riddled n' rhythmed with life;

just whisper My name or shout—it's the same,
for I am inside the dark and the light,

and if you forget, dearest, know I won't chide;
no, beloved, I'll never leave your side."

In some green bower
Rest, and be not alone, but have thou there
The One who is thy choice of all the world:
There linger, listening, gazing, with delight…

Be hallowed, love that breathes not without awe;
Love that adores, but on the knees of prayer,
By heaven inspired; that frees for chains the soul,
Lifted, in union with the purest, best,
Of earth-born passions, on the wings of praise
Bearing a tribute to the Almighty's Throne.

> - William Wordsworth,
> *The Prelude – Book VI:*
> *Cabridge and the Alps*

Prelude: The Spring

There are places we visit again and again—memories and faces therein take on a distinct flavor and fragrance in our souls; some bitter, others potent with grace. Memories wake us to who we are and shape where we're going; the most significant ones mark our souls forever. Jesus spoke of rivers of Living Water that flow from the hearts of those who come to Him. I wonder if our memories with Him can bubble up too, like an everlasting spring in our souls and flood our being and our world with life?

> But when I look down, a new wonder met my view....beneath the wave, I floated above my whole Past. The fields of my childhood flitted by; the halls of my youthful labors; the streets of great cities where I had dwelt; and the assemblies of men and women wherein I had wearied myself seeking for rest....In dreams of unspeakable joy—of restored friendships; of revived embraces; of love which said it had never died; of faces that had vanished long ago, yet said with smiling lips that they knew nothing of the grave; of pardons implored, and granted with such bursting floods of love, that I was almost glad I had sinned—thus I passed through this wondrous twilight…feeling I had been kissed and loved to my heart's content.
>
> - George MacDonald, *Phantastes*

The Spring

i asked about the pond we found
a little further from the house
than i'd been all my life.
it was full even in drought
my father'd said,
and so clear
even with the glare.

i could see it was deep—
and i ran through the grass that came
to the edge
to look
but i slipped
and my foot sunk in and my elbow too.

i reached for grass and pulled myself out,
breathed deep,
then sighed,
then laughed at myself
and stood (with shirt off),
and backed away to get some distance.

i ran to the edge (full speed)—took a leap,
                plugged my nose,
                        breathed deep
                                closed my eyes.

i went back every day.

: :

i dropped my bags: (there were two).
hugged my dad.
kicked my shoes.
threw my shirt.

in the sun my eyes glared
but i lifted my hand and jogged
through the grass
and sat my feet in
to cool awhile.

i paused and decided
rolled backward and stood.
i braced myself
and jumped.

: :

this time i landed: briefcase and tie,
hugged my dad
and we sat and talked for a while.

i took off my shoes,
leaned back on the couch,
placed my hands behind my head
and let my sigh out.

it was dark when i stepped into the kitchen
late that night,
opened the fridge,
glancing in, but nothing looked good—

so i sipped filtered water,

walked upstairs,
and told my eyes to close.

they shot open quick! like white light
through the window
i yanked open the blinds
and looked across the field.

threw on my robe,
ran out to the shed
grabbed a shovel and a pickaxe
(and glad that I did).

i quickened myself to the edge of the water,
took my shovel and pickaxe
and began to dig wider

i tore the grass, i threw the dirt in a heap,
breathing heavy with every wide sweep.

after hours hands blistered raw and sore
i sat on my robe in the dirt and sobbed.

        i stood up   and   i   dug.
           i sat   and   i   wept.
        i stood   to   dig   again,

        but i couldn't stand anymore.

so i crawled myself to the edge of the pool,
saw the dirt on my hands
and my face and my hair
(even my teeth and my tongue

and my smile)
as i kneeled i closed my eyes

and slipped my hands in the water,
rubbed them slowly together,
as a cloud appeared
and disappeared forever.

      i took off my robe
        i washed off my toes
     in measure i paused
       breathed

and slipped myself deep,

       deep,

          deep.

         it enveloped me.

     : :

i was older and further: heavy hearted, suspended
i wept for my father with my face in my hands
and my hands in the water.

it held me complete,
 —in its depths

i go farther.

: :

now i spend my days at the home of my youth.
many mornings i wake and walk out to our pond.

sometimes my eyes open in the glare of the dawn
i'm still in the water—still sinking deeper,
seeing the surface,
watching the lights flicker—
they dance on the edge
like leaves in the wind
and wish to look in,
and be as deep as i.

    and i just smile
    and sink
    and smile.

Jesus, let the power of your word
flow free among us,
we are your community,
and you are abundant;

so what-ever, though we lose,
though we pine and die,
Lord, what-ever, let it be stripped
and gone inside Your light.

Lord, whatever also, ah,
in that season only you know,
let us fly into your arms,
let your presence hold us close.

our hearts were sown in sweet surrender,
and still, oh they flutter so,
take the worst and best in us,
let us become the word you know.

Jesus, help us put You on,
and through entire years,
let wear You as a garment
of our laughter and our tears.

we are fully who we are in You,
and to this You only know,
please Jesus pour Your Spirit out,
it's in You we place our hope.

Everything else in meaningless,
it's in You we've placed our hope.

Meaning & Sound

Poems are made up of words that create meaning and sound. The sound of the word must be vocalized in mouth or in thought. That sound carries an innate meaning: an idea, experience or memory.

For example, a word like mug, for me, carries the *meaning* of a warm drink, friendship and reflection— arising from definition, but also from experience. Regarding *sound*, mug has a soft m, (mmm), and a long u, (uhhh), and a softer form of the letter g (gh rather then jee). Contrast "mug" to "cup." Though their meanings are close, cup has a shorter, sharper sound, a bit harsher, and ends with a sharp "p."

These word choices create the art and pleasure of poetry. Sound and meaning create a poet's canvas and words become paint in the reader's ear. To appreciate poetry, one needs to develop an appreciation for the innate palate of sound and meaning in everyday language[7].

---

[7] ideas for Meaning & Sound are borrowed from Mary Oliver, *A Poetry Handbook*'

Take a moment to consider:

- What words or phrases stand out in these poems?

- What word-sounds catch your ear?

- What is your sense of the author's meaning?

- What does each poem mean to you?

Experience, Mood & Emotion

Poets use the meaning and sounds of words to create a *mood* through our common experience. Take the phrase, "A tall, nonfat, triple-shot latte's ready at the bar." This everyday quip contains a lot of quick-sounding words, with clear meanings. For me, the mood of this phrase seems fast, direct, harsh, and even a bit impersonal. And for the poet, communicating that experience is central.

Poets paint with language through phrases and scenes that attempt to coax out common *experience*. The best poetry articulates the experience of the heart. Enjoyment, beauty, and connection grasp the reader when the poet enfleshes in language something true in the reader's experience. The words tap into our common humanity, communicating for the reader what before may have been inexpressible.

Mood carries with it an *emotion*. The phrase, "Come here, Darling," with its soft consonants and almost melodic sound can signify for many the comforting invitation of a caretaker. To me, it sounds like safety, peace, even touch. While reading, I may begin to feel a longing to be comforted or recall a memory of someone's tangible care. The descriptors one uses may differ from person to person, but the experience, the mood, the emotion remains as the locus of our formation.

Take a moment to consider:

- What common experience stands out to you in these poems? How would you describe the mood?

- What emotion do you think the poet is feeling? As you read, what are you feeling?

- Remember, the poet is writing about experience, so the meaning can remain largely relative without losing the meaning of that experience. It is important to consider what experience this poem surfaces for *you*.

Listening

Lastly, *listening* is the virtue cultivated through poetry. Learning to hear a poem at heart-level and receive nourishment from those words is a powerful activator for personal and relational growth.

This practice of poetical listening creates hospitality—the poem becomes a place where self-reflection, honesty, and emotion are welcome. Hospitality and its gifts can overflow into a rich, meaning-filled, integrated life, if only we take time to listen.

Take a moment to consider:

- What is most deeply resonating with *you* about these poems?

- What do these poems have to do with *your* life, who *you* are, who *you've* been, and who *you* are becoming?

- Share these insights with someone safe.

ABOUT THE AUTHOR

David is a poet at heart, writing stories and devotional poetry for over 15 years. He has always delighted in the sounds and meanings of words mingling together, moving the soul as a symphony. For David, poetry is a place of discovery where he can express his heart while deepening and growing his relationship with God. David and his wife, Keri, live in the Santa Cruz Mountains. She more than anyone in his life has encouraged him toward the journey of writing. He couldn't have done this without her.

If you enjoy these poems please visit:
DavidMichaelLippman.com

 Facebook.com/DavidMichaelLippman

 @David_Michael_Lippman

Made in the USA
Middletown, DE
18 February 2019